D0784959

THE
ANSWERS

LUCY KELLAWAY is the management columnist at the *Financial Times* and is well known for her pointed commentaries on the limitations of modern corporate culture. She was named Columnist of the Year at the British Press Awards in 2006, and is the author of *Sense and Nonsense in the Office* and *Martin Lukes: Who Moved My BlackBerry*. She lives in London with her husband and four children.

THE
ANSWERS

All the office questions
you never dared to ask

LUCY KELLAWAY

P

PROFILE BOOKS

First published in Great Britain in 2007 by
Profile Books Ltd
3A Exmouth House
Pine Street
London
ECIR OJH
www.profilebooks.com

3 5 7 9 10 8 6 4 2

Typeset in Plantin by MacGuru Ltd
info@macguru.org.uk
Designed by Sue Lamble
Printed and bound in Great Britain by
Clays, Bungay, Suffolk

A CIP catalogue record for this book is available from the British Library.

ISBN 978 1 84668 039 7

The paper this book is printed on is certified by the © 1996 Forest
Stewardship Council A.C. (FSC). It is ancient-forest friendly. The printer
holds FSC chain of custody SGS-COC-2061

FSC
Mixed Sources
Product group from well-managed
forests and other controlled sources

Cert no. SGS-COC-2061
www.fsc.org
© 1996 Forest Stewardship Council

Contents

INTRODUCTION

I always wanted to be an agony aunt. There may have been a brief period when I was about nine during which I flirted with the idea of being an air hostess instead, but by the time I was thirteen my ambition was strong and unwavering. I wanted to write a column in a magazine giving out advice to readers.

My favourite reading matter at that age was *Jackie*, a teen magazine all about Donny Osmond and midi-skirts. The best part was the problem page on which Cathy & Claire meted out straight-talking advice to tortured adolescents. When readers wrote in moaning about their two-timing boyfriends, Cathy & Claire would briskly tell them to stop being doormats.

As I got older I started to show promise as the sort of person that people came to for direction. Soon after I joined the *Financial Times* twenty years ago, my colleague Dominic Lawson (son of the former chancellor of the exchequer, he went on to edit the *Spectator* and the *Sunday Telegraph*) matter-of-factly informed me that I had a 'lavatory face'.

This did not sound terribly nice, but then Dominic often said things that were not nice. He went on to explain that I, like his mother, had the kind of face someone coming into an office full of strangers would instinctively turn to for directions to the lavatory.

It might not have been much, but it was a start. In fact, not only did I confidently tell people the most direct route to the office loo, but as time went on I started dispensing more complicated advice too.

Eventually, at the beginning of 2006, some thirty-five years after I hatched the plan, it came to pass. My agony column started to appear on Wednesdays in the *FT* and since then I have handed out advice on bullying bosses, office affairs, sexism, when to wear chinos: big problems, little problems.

In dispensing workplace advice, I've joined a crowded market. You might say there are too many peddlers of 'solutions' already – with all those executive coaches and trainers and 'facilitators'. But most of them offer advice based on fashionable theories of management, most of which is daft. My USP is that I have no fashionable theories. I never mention comfort zones, though if I did I would never, ever recommend stepping outside one. In my experience comfort is nice, and hard to achieve. If you have managed to get comfortable, I would strongly recommend that you keep up the good work. In truth I have no theories at all, except that working life can be hard and we must muddle through as best we can.

My only qualification for handing out advice (apart from a desire to do so) is that I have worked in offices for a quarter of a century. I have written and read about the problems of office life for nearly as long (as well as experienced a good few difficulties myself) and I offer a humbug-free service, with all my answers written in a few easy-to-understand words.

A second differentiating feature is that I'm not frightened of the negative. Most agony aunts and other advice providers now refer to problems as 'dilemmas'; the word sounds less negative and, in this self-improving world, we have to be positive at all costs. By contrast, my problems are called just that – problems – because that is what they are, and because working life is stuffed full with them. The more negative and intractable the problem, the more satisfaction I get from thinking about it and trying to solve it.

The first thing people want to know when I say I'm an agony aunt is whether the problems are real, or whether they have been whisked up by me in an idle moment. The answer is that they are all real. Though that doesn't mean that they all reach me in the conventional way. Only about half the problems in this book arrived obediently via the problems inbox (problems@ft.com, in case you have something you'd like to submit); the rest had to be winkled out.

When I first put an invitation in the *FT* soliciting for agony, I received a great many responses – which was good. What was less good was that some readers did not understand quite what sort of problem I was after.

One man wrote asking if I could help him with off-street parking in the Essex village where he lives. The answer to this was no, I could not. Another person sent in a question about why the *FT* charges for access to a lot of FT.com material. I can answer this, although I do not consider it a problem as such. The reason is that the *FT* is a business, and therefore it is trying to make money.

In addition to these there were some pukka problems that were just what I was after. In that very first crop there was a man jaded from his job as a City lawyer and wedded to a (dotty, in my view) search for more meaningful work. There was a woman whose colleague had been convicted of downloading child porn and who, on his release from prison, had tried to get in touch with her again.

Though the problems that I'm sent are plentiful, there is a snag. They don't cover the waterfront. There is no shortage of emails from people with troublesome bosses or colleagues or from middle-aged professionals finding out that working life is not quite what they hoped it would be. But nothing from bosses. I'm never sent problems about the hard things senior managers have to do: firing people or promoting them or motivating them. This is sad, though not surprising. It isn't that bosses don't have problems: obviously they do. It is that unless they are slightly odd, bosses simply don't write to newspaper agony aunts begging for advice.

So I have had to be what is popularly called 'proactive' in flushing out problems. Every time I meet anyone I start probing. I ask managers what is troubling them most at the moment (apart from the fact that a middle-aged woman with a glint in her eye is asking prying questions). If they tell me something that sounds interesting I write it up.

This has got me into difficulties in the past. I should apologise to the person who told me that his boss hit him. He seemed pleased when I said I was going to use his story as a problem, indeed he had told everyone in his office to look out for it. He was less pleased when he read the answer, in which I suggested that his male boss might fancy him. It seems I was wide of the mark – or perhaps I was painfully close to the truth. Either way, it went down badly, and I apologise sincerely for any embarrassment caused.

From the beginning I knew that I was going to need some help in answering the problems. Even great agony aunts sometimes give out duff advice, so it is a good idea to have some back-up. Cathy & Claire themselves were not infallible: my thirteen-year-old mind baulked at the idea that a girl worried about her kissing skills should start to practise by kissing the back of her own hand.

To avoid such pitfalls I invited *FT* readers to submit their own answers to problems and promised to print the best. I had no idea what sort of response I would get. I was hoping to hear from people who had had similar experiences to the problems in question, which I did, sometimes in large numbers. When I printed a problem from someone who was concerned that a friendship with a female colleague was getting dangerous, the response was an emotional outpouring of angst and intimacy revealing a whole new side to *FT* readers. It seemed that getting into hot water with female colleagues was the most common thing in the world, and the unanimous advice they offered was DON'T.

Even more surprising are the number of readers who turn out to be closet agony aunts themselves. While bosses might not like admitting to their own problems, they certainly like pronouncing on other people's.

From the start I decided it would be better not to put names on the readers' replies. This is partly because I have often had to be brutal in cutting over-long responses, whose authors might prefer to disown the butchered version, but mainly because people who are tempted to tell the world what they've learnt from their disastrous office affairs and humiliating sackings appreciate a little anonymity.

Instead I identify people only by sex, age and profession. Some readers have complained that this makes them feel like lab rats, but that is precisely why I like the system. It makes it sound scientific, which it isn't really – though it does test one's prejudices. What I like most is receiving crusty, no-nonsense advice and find it is written not by a retired male director of sixty-five but by a twenty-five-year-old woman in PR.

So after a year and a half on the job, have I found that being an agony aunt lives up to my dream? Yes and no. The problems (now that I know how to procure them) have been juicier and altogether more varied than I had expected. A month or two after the column started, one senior colleague solemnly took me to one side to say that it might be OK so far, but I wouldn't be able to sustain it as I'd soon run out of problems.

Once I had done bullying and sacking and office affairs, there wouldn't be anything left.

He was quite wrong. It seems to me that the supply of problems is close to endless. That is because, in addition to predictable ones, there are lots of unpredictable one-offs: the PR man who is certain that the cleaner has nicked his trainers, but has no proof; the man who has got into a terrible tangle with his PA over her plans for cosmetic surgery. These problems are my favourites: quaint and unexpected as well as being morally interesting. Each, in its small way, pitches what is pragmatic and sensible against what is right or kind. They test one's humanity.

However, slowly I am beginning to wonder about the supremacy of my replies. As I sit down to draft my know-all answers I usually feel an agreeable glow of confidence that my solution is the right one. Yet when I read through the readers' replies I can't help noticing that each one seems equally sure of the wisdom of their own advice, most of which is quite different from mine, and from each other's.

One might have thought that thriving in business means behaving in certain predictable ways. This book shows the opposite to be true. Most of my correspondents have been quite – or even very – successful, yet there are few common denominators in their behaviour, ambitions or world views at all.

You might say this defeats the purpose of having a column like mine: if there are no right answers, what is the point of producing any answers at all? And faced with so many wildly conflicting opinions, the person seeking advice surely will not emerge as a satisfied customer but will simply have their original problem compounded by a splitting headache.

Actually there *are* right answers, but they depend on the personality of the person asking. Conflicting advice can be helpful in making people know their own mind: reading something you don't agree with can be even more helpful than reading something you do. Indeed, when I come across advice from readers that is diametrically opposed to my own, it usually makes me even more devoted to my view than I was beforehand.

Finally, a word on my classification system. First, I have sorted the problems according to subject matter. This was quite easy, though I have taken a few liberties, squeezing problems into categories where they don't quite fit. The man who has panic attacks before speeches doesn't really belong in 'Office Life', but there was nowhere better to put him, and I didn't want to leave him out.

I have also graded the problems against two scores: angst and difficulty. By 'angst' I mean how horrible the problem makes its owner feel. By 'difficulty' I mean how hard the problem is to solve. Mostly the two go together. When a young woman on Wall Street asks, 'Do I dare to take a lunch break?' the problem is fairly low in angst, and also low in difficulty. The answer, in my view, is no. By contrast, the woman who has to share an office with the man she has had an affair with, scores up to the maximum on both angst and difficulty. Hers is a miserable situation, and there is no easy solution to it as far as I can see.

However, some problems score high on one measure and low on another. The boss who has an employee with BO is probably suffering from fairly low angst levels, even if the smell is truly rancid. Yet the difficulty rating is high: telling someone they stink is one of the least enviable tasks a manager might have to undertake.

Reading through the problems in this book, I think I come over as unsentimental to a fault. Work is a way of earning money, and a good enough job is the best that most of us will ever get. To the people who agonise about following their dreams, I caution that reality is a better bet than dreams, and you get more money for it too.

Which brings me back to the beginning. How come I am following my dream in becoming an agony aunt when I nearly always advise other people not to follow theirs? Partly it is because my dream is an addition to what I do already: I have not given up the day job. But it is also because of the agony aunt's greatest secret: you can spend all day telling people to be wise, good, sensible and hard working, while at the same time reserving the right to be sometimes unwise, bad, silly and sloppy yourself.

BOSSES

' How do I persuade my boss to stop hitting me? '

ANGST ✱✲✲✲✲
DIFFICULTY ✱✱✲✲✲

I love where I work but have an ongoing issue with my boss. Every so often, as a joke and usually for something trivial, he hits me – not with his fist, of course, but with a rolled-up newspaper or a book – and although it's in jest it strikes me as inappropriate, and occasionally leaves bruises. I wouldn't want to bring this up in case it escalates into anything more serious, but what can I do? He doesn't do it to anyone else. I think it is a sign of favouritism. We really do get on well, and I don't want to spoil that.

Editorial director, male, 30

THE ANSWER

When I was eight I had a piano teacher who used to hit me in jest. He would punch my arm in slow motion, exclaiming, 'My dear girl!' It wasn't painful, but I didn't like it.

This was partly because I was tiny and he was enormous, but also because there was a suppressed violence to it. I was bad at playing the piano, and the mannered punch felt like a substitute for what he surely wanted to do – to beat me to a pulp for my halting version of 'Für Elise'. I couldn't tell him to stop because I was a child, and children didn't tell off adults in those days.

Your case is different. You are not eight, although your message makes you sound as if you might be. Your boss doesn't think you are useless, he thinks you are great. If you get on well, you should be able to say, 'Please don't do that.' Given that he sometimes hits you hard (your mention of bruises is a little alarming), you could simply squeal 'Ow! That hurt!' Surely that should do the trick.

Your fear that bringing it up could make things 'escalate into something more serious' makes me uneasy. What did you have in mind? Surely the worst thing that could happen is that he would think you a wimp, which wouldn't be the end of the world.

Also odd is your acknowledgement that the whacks are a sign of favouritism, and that you don't want to spoil that. Favouritism that expresses itself in blows doesn't sound like something worth preserving.

It's possible that the blows are a clumsy attempt at flirtation. If that's the case, you should definitely say something now – if you continue to laugh along, you may find you have a bigger problem on your hands.

DOWN, BOY!

My lively Labrador puppy used to jump up and attack my genitals every time I came home. My solution: I feigned great pain and fell to the floor, making noises of agony. He had his tail between his legs for the rest of the evening and never

jumped up again. Next time let your boss know how much it hurts.
Unemployed, male, 49

PREGNANT PAWS

Hit him back, hard. When I was pregnant I hated people putting their hands on my belly, so I'd put my hand on theirs whenever they did. They soon got the message.
Aid worker, female, 30s

LITTLE WONDER

Do you make a habit of turning simple issues into moral dilemmas worthy of Dostoyevsky? No wonder people want to smack you in the head. The next time you see your boss playfully hefting a newspaper or book, look him in the eye and say, 'Don't hit me with that. Because I don't actually like it.' Then he won't hit you with it any more.
Director, male, 37

GET IN TRAINING

It's not only inappropriate. It could be battery, actionable without having to prove damages. But if you really savour this favouritism, I suggest you get some training. Next time, react swiftly, catching his arm before it reaches you. You will then look cool and smart.
Law student, male, 21

SHIELD YOURSELF

Buy a replica of a medieval knight's shield. Carry the shield around and block his books and papers with it. You will look ridiculous and he will question why you would carry such a silly thing around the office. Respond in a humorous way that

you are trying to protect your body from physical harm. He
will realise how silly he is for hitting you in jest.
Dreamer, male, 30

❝ How do I manage this young whippersnapper boss? ❞

ANGST ✷✷✷✷✷
DIFFICULTY ✷✷✷✷✷

I have recently acquired a new boss who is
thirty-two. I am twenty years older and consider
myself not just more experienced but considerably
better educated and more intelligent. I am having
great difficulty working for someone so young whom
I don't respect. He has had many hare-brained ideas
and to my disgust all my colleagues are kowtowing
to him. I fear I may already have alienated him
by pointing out that some of his schemes won't
fly. Do you have any advice on how I manage this
whippersnapper?

Manager, male, 51

THE ANSWER

Before I tell you what I think of your problem, I should
warn you that most *FT* readers under forty (a few over forty)
hold you in contempt. According to their e-mails, you are a
ghastly old git in denial that someone better than you is now

your boss. Like most of the *FT*'s older readers, I don't think you are a ghastly git at all. In fact, I can easily imagine feeling the same way myself.

Having someone twenty years younger as a boss is hard – it is the final confirmation that you are way over the hill, and it is quite reasonable that one should mind about that. In a politically correct office we are expected to be age-blind, but age remains a big part of where we feel we fit into a hierarchy and it is silly to pretend otherwise. What is happening to you will come to us all, and we will all have to learn to put up with it – but that doesn't make it pleasant.

As for the supposed uselessness of your young boss, I can believe he is less experienced and more ignorant than you. Many of his generation are. However, he may have other qualities that make him a better manager – or he may not. It wouldn't be the first time a fool got over-promoted.

Still, whether or not he actually deserves the job is beside the point. You have been foolish to offend him, and you must row back sharpish.

As I can't see you landing a peachy job outside, you can either stick it out gracefully or become a grumpy nuisance. The latter would be silly because it will put your job at risk, and because by obsessing about him you'll end up bitter and boring – an old git, in fact.

Without kowtowing, you should concentrate on doing your own job well. The passing of time will help, and not just because it will get you nearer to a pension, which I assume is your end game. His schemes may get less hare brained, and you will slowly get used to the shocking sight of his fresh face.

A final point: the word whippersnapper is a favourite of mine. It is deliciously evocative. My advice that I give with lingering regret: avoid.

OLD GIT 1

It seems to me you're just jealous of his success. I'm young myself and very intelligent, but have already learnt that there will always be someone brighter and younger than me. I can live with that and I'm surprised that you, in your fifties, cannot.

Banker, male, 23

OLD GIT 2

Every word you use screams 'obnoxious, negative employee with no contribution to offer'. Your company clearly has good reason to promote someone twenty years younger over you. Either you change your attitude and contribute to the success of your team by humbly offering any wisdom your extra twenty years have given you, or get out before you are fired for your shockingly negative attitude.

CIO, male, 40s

AGEIST GIT

Imagine if your boss was someone of a sex, race or religion for whom you found it difficult to work. Substitute 'whippersnapper' for your chosen sexist or racist epithet and then imagine how many job interviews you can cram into your sudden abundance of free time.

Banker, male, 43

HELP HIM SUCCEED

You are not a team player, you are difficult to manage and you have a bad attitude. Either give your boss the benefit of the doubt or find a new job.

Manager, female, 27

HELP HIM FAIL

Support all his ideas to the hilt. That way he'll come a cropper sooner. The more unobtrusively you do it, the better – you won't be implicated when he finally overreaches, but will be better placed when he goes down.
Academic, female, 40s

MAKE THE BEST OF IT

I am the same age as you and in a similar situation. Our promotion prospects are finished, so we must swallow our pride and defuse our ambition. Tell your boss you'll be loyal. Work for him in areas where he is weak – he'll take the credit, but he'll defend you as he needs you. You can enjoy your life without the stress of managerial bureaucracy.
Banker, male, 52

THE LAST LAUGH

Remember: cunning and treachery vanquish youth and enthusiasm.
Manager, male, 55

‘My new boss thinks I'm a waste of space’

ANGST *****

DIFFICULTY *****

The chief executive of the company where I work has just been fired. He was my mentor, and under him I have been rapidly promoted to a senior position. The new chief executive is someone I've worked with for a long time. He is very political and has his favourites. I've had a couple of run-ins with him in the past, and I fear he neither likes me nor rates me. Clearly my job is now very vulnerable – he may want to give it to someone else. My problem is that I don't want to leave; I like the work and the culture and the money's good. What can I do to convince him that I'm worth keeping? Doing great work won't achieve that – I do great work anyway and he has never valued it. I don't think being smarmy is going to work either. Any ideas?

Manager, male, 37

THE ANSWER

Things are looking irredeemably grim for you. Your new boss will be choosing his new team even as I write this, and chances are you won't be on it. He neither likes nor rates you and there's little you can do to change that. Don't even think of going to see him and telling him how great you are. He'd still think you hopeless, but would put you down as a pain and a bragger too.

Your best hope is that for some political reason he finds getting rid of you is more problematic than keeping you. If so, you'll have more time to work on him. You are right that working hard is unlikely to impress him: in my experience good work always goes undetected by a boss intent on seeing your flaws.

Smarmy might work better, though it is difficult to bring off. It only succeeds when done in precisely the way that individual likes best. It sounds as if you are the last person to be able to get this right with him.

You say he doesn't rate or like you, but do you rate or like him? I get the strong impression you don't. This means that setting out to please him may turn your stomach – and make you wonder if the effort is worth it.

So even if you survive the first cut, you are not going to do well or be happy for as long as he stays chief executive. Maybe you reason that he'll be fired soon and that you can hang on until then. If that's your strategy, next time you must obey the fundamental law of political organisations: one mentor is not enough.

All this is probably hypothetical, as I daresay you'll be out on your ear soon. So start looking for another job today, but don't do anything hasty. It would be a mistake to jump before you are pushed. The great thing about being pushed is that you tend to get paid handsomely for the privilege.

TALKING CURE

Confront him. Explain your concerns and tell him that you think you are doing great work but feel he doesn't think you are; is this the case? If he says yes, how can you address it? You should also keep in contact with your old chief executive. He may resurface and want to do the age-old cop-out of surrounding himself with sycophants.

Director, male, 58

WAITING GAME

You are fortunate to have a well-paying job that you enjoy. Perhaps it would be best if you just stay put, get on with your work and see what happens.

Analyst, female, 46

BEEN THERE

I have had a similar problem three times running, while working for that ultimate example of internal politics and the power of patronage – a French bank. My first solution was to follow my mentor to his new position. The second time, when my boss again moved, I negotiated an early change of employment. Finally, I endured the third, new and unsupportive chief executive for several months until successfully negotiating a decent cheque to go home.

Ex-banker, male, 53

YOU'RE DOOMED

The situation has happened to me twice and both times I did not fare well. The first time I was made 'redundant' – my new boss's assistant got my job. The second time I ended up as the

'quality, safety and environmental manager' – a non-job if ever there was one.
Manager, male, 49

BROWNED OFF

Exactly which member of the Cabinet is it who is asking?
Coach, male, 54

'My ageing boss is a slacker who won't quit'

ANGST ✱✱✱✱✱
DIFFICULTY ✱✱✱✱✱

I'm a professional in my fifties with a boss who is nearly seventy. Though I want him to retire for my own advancement, that is not the most pressing problem. It is that he has stopped pulling his weight, is coming in late, leaving early and taking too much holiday. This puts an extra burden on the team, but especially on me as the right-hand man. His superiors don't seem to notice, and to tell them would make me seem disloyal and overly ambitious. He's in exceptionally good health and could work for several more years. Should I confront my boss or just keep mum?

Banker, male, 52

THE ANSWER

How delightful to find an arriviste underling of fifty-two and a slacking boss of seventy in a thrusting, ageist industry such as investment banking.

Yet maybe this is the future: ten years from now everyone will go on working into their dotage because they won't be able to afford to retire. And many of them will, like your boss, spend their last decade skiving as there will no longer be any point in working like a maniac – and they will deserve a breather anyway. The trouble, as you have found, is that the tier below will feel put-upon and restive.

As for the specifics of your problem, you ask if you should take your boss aside and tell him he's coasting. This is such a terrible idea I find it hard to believe you have ever entertained it. How do you think he'd feel on being told off by you? He certainly wouldn't work harder and would only conclude that, despite your relatively advanced age, you were still a petty little school prefect.

I think you are looking at your problem in the wrong way. You clearly want his job, yet realise you aren't going to get it any time soon. But actually you already have the job, in that you are doing most of the work. So the real question is not how to get your skiving boss to do his job, but how to get recognition for the bits of it that you are now doing on an unpaid basis.

I suggest you do this in two stages. First, make sure you are doing the extra stuff publicly, willingly and well. Then go and see your boss's bosses and tell them what's what. Make sure you sound happy to be doing the work (i.e., no moaning) and also make clear that you respect your boss and are grateful for any advice he continues to hand down from above. Then insist on more money, and possibly a souped-up title.

I am slightly worried by your assumption that you will be promoted when your boss finally does decide to cultivate his roses.

By then you may be getting on a bit too, and possibly someone much younger will be put in over your head. Life can be horrid that way.

YOU'RE NOT THE MAN

You are aged fifty-plus and your boss's right-hand man? Yet you are still unable to talk to him about his understandable rebalancing of his work life in the twilight of his career? It sounds as if you are not the right person to succeed him and that his superiors have already come to that conclusion. Stand by for a new boss from outside the company.

CEO, male, 50

STARVE HIM OUT

Marginalise him. Have no work waiting for him, do not call him when he's away and do not keep him up to date. When he's out of the loop his bosses will start to think he's going senile. He'll be 'retired' in months. For the next couple of years you're free. Anything that goes wrong, blame him, and anything that goes well, take full credit. But be careful of that thirty-five-year-old who's looking at your job.

Trader, male, 35

HE'S USING YOU

I have experienced the same problem. My boss promised me and one other colleague he would lobby hard for our promotions on his retirement. He dumped all of his work on us and coasted to retirement without acting on the promotions. Learn from our mistake. Either confront your boss about pulling his own weight or seek the higher position you desire elsewhere. He is using you and your team and enjoying the free ride.

Manager, male, 40

YIN AND YANG

Like you, I am a 'chef de cabinet' with the CEO of a bank who is nearly seventy. He has given the day-to-day business to me and I benefit from his accumulated experience when I need it. I see the relationship as like that between a management and supervisory board. My boss is pleased with a comfortable situation that gives him the satisfaction of still being useful – and so am I.

Banker, male, 50s

YOUR BOSS'S SECRET

Your boss's age is a red herring. He has found a new love of thirty-something and is having the time of his life with the help of modern pharmaceuticals. Have empathy and patience. One day when you are a senior partner you may find yourself in a similar position. Just keep fit.

Male, retired, 66

‘I think my boss may be bipolar’

ANGST ✳✳✳✳✳
DIFFICULTY ✳✳✳✳✳

I think my boss may be bipolar. He has two different modes: he's either charging round, full of energy, making bold decisions or he's paranoid, negative and bullying. In the 'up' moods he's stimulating, though it's exhausting trying to keep up. The rest of the time he is paranoid and hostile. I've worked for him for two years and though I admire his talent and charisma I find his mood swings increasingly stressful. A couple of weeks ago I tried to broach the matter, but he looked as if he was about to have a coronary, so I shut up. Is there anything I can do? And if not, how can I insulate myself from the worst of his rages?

Investment banker, male, 36

THE ANSWER

You are in very good company. So many readers have sent in messages saying that their boss is as erratic and as bonkers as yours that it makes one wonder if there are any normal, stable, easygoing ones around – especially in investment banking.

There are two reasons why there are so many nutters in these jobs. People who make it to the top of competitive industries are hardly ever well balanced, as well-balanced people tend not to strive so hard. And even if they started off normal, the stress, the glory and the power of doing these jobs can make them demented or lead them to seek further thrills in cocaine (or similar) – which makes them more demented still. As far as your boss goes he may have been born like that, the job may have brought it on, or he might be perfectly OK if only he stopped snorting so much coke.

While it might be interesting in theory to know which of the three was the problem, from your point of view it may not make much difference. That is because there isn't much you can do. As you discovered, confronting him is pointless and dangerous and utterly not to be recommended. You just about got away with it once: next time, instead of having a coronary, he might chop your head off.

The obvious answer would be to find someone else in the company you could go to for help. The fact that you haven't done this suggests there isn't a benign boss above him. You could turn to HR, though to expect an HR lackey to have sway over a master of the universe is not very realistic.

If he is as bad as you say, and particularly if the problem is drugs, he will get fired eventually, though it may take time. In the meantime you have to insulate yourself from his moods. I suggest you constantly tell yourself that he is mad, bad and dangerous to know. Laugh at his ways behind his back with your colleagues. Every time he does something horrendous, think how much you will enjoy retelling it as an anecdote later on. And while you are laughing, keep an eye on the job ads –

though bear in mind you may not find your new boss is any better.

PUT HIM IN A BOX

I am battling the same issue. I manage the problem by: (1) just accepting that her poor interpersonal skills mean she will never really understand why her unpredictable moods are a problem for us; and (2) in my head she lives in a 'box' and I only allow her out of that box in office hours – this has stopped me stressing about her out of office hours so makes the problem manageable. Interestingly this method was given to me by her boss, who faces the same problem with her!
Banker, male, 30s

GET OUT NOW

I had a boss who was very similar – she ended up driving me into depression. The situation may not get any better and this can have an impact on you.

The lack of rationality that you have to cope with can put enough mental pressure on you that it causes you to question your judgement and eventually you follow the mood swings.

That's good for no one. Get out as soon as you can.
Manager, female, 40

COKE HEAD

Sounds like a coke problem to me. Bipolar people aren't paranoid and bullying in their down phases – they're usually apathetic and totally non-functional. Also be secure in the knowledge that in a couple more years he'll crash and burn in a blaze of septum-ruptured glory – leaving you, the survivor, to the spoils.
PR, female, 25

HE'S MY BOSS TOO

Do we have the same boss? My tuppence worth from the City
trenches: try to keep out of his way, try only to report success
and watch the sits-vac ads.
Banker, male, 30s

HAT TRICK

I've worked closely with three people like this. The first died
(brain tumour), the second was, I'm reasonably sure, taking
drugs and the third was stress related. I've learnt that if you
try to use reason with people who enjoy confrontation, it
makes things worse. When the stress of dealing with a person
like this is greater than the rewards, it is time to move on.
Handing in your resignation could be a catalyst to sorting it
out with your boss, if he appreciates you. If he doesn't, you are
definitely doing the right thing by resigning.
Director, male, 58

PLASTIC BOSS

Which kind of boss would you rather have: a real person who
has moods or somebody who walks around all day with a
smile painted on his face, calling your problems 'challenges'
and facing everything with the same robotic demeanour? If
you'd rather work for a cartoon character, I suggest a job at
Euro Disney. Or Silicon Valley.
Director, male, 38

❝ My boss is an out-and-out bully; what can I do? ❞

ANGST ✳✳✳✳✳

DIFFICULTY ✳✳✳✳✳

I recently started working at a political risk consultancy. It is my first job and it was a big coup to get it. However, I find the chief executive is a tyrant. He is pedantic, condescending and patronising and almost every day criticises me in front of colleagues. I am in a probation period and have been warned that if I do not show due deference to him I will be sacked at the end of it.

This is a clear case of bullying, but the company is small and has no human-resources department. I have discovered that a number of people have left due to mental and physical health issues. I am also worried that if I leave it will look bad on my CV. What shall I do?

Consultant, female, 20s

THE ANSWER

Your problem has moved many readers to express compassion for you and rage at your tyrannical boss. Before you read some of their responses, I want to give you my less sympathetic advice: grow a thick skin and put up with the bully – at least for now.

I take it you have an analytical mind otherwise you would not have landed this job. That should help you see beyond the hysteria about bullying, which rates it as one of the greatest workplace crimes. Being bullied is not fun, but you should try to rise above that and look dispassionately at your options.

First, you could leave. You fear this would look bad on your CV, though I think the true risk in quitting is not the signal it sends to future employers but the signal it sends to you, the novice employee. You need to learn that work is hard, and that bosses can be dreadful (bullying is only one of many popular shortcomings).

The second option would be to confront him. As you point out, you have no HR department (though I am touched at your faith that HR departments are good at dealing with this sort of thing anyway). So you'd have to stand up to him yourself – which would be as brave as it would be stupid. The sort of tyrant who roughs up his young hires is not the sort to respond kindly when they point out how bad his behaviour is.

Finally, you could shut up and stay. The danger is that you could end up a mental wreck. But why should that happen? This is not personal – your boss is horrible to everyone. And you say it usually gets better after six months. Surely even at your age that isn't a long time. So stay, and learn something from him (you don't say if he's smart as well as horrid, but I suspect he is).

You could also laugh behind his back with the other people he has bullied. If things do not get better after six months then write to me again – and I might try to be a little bit nicer.

GET OUT 1

Life is too short to tolerate situations like this. Tell him to get stuffed. Your self-respect is far too important to compromise at such an early stage of your working life.

It is only when one has a mortgage, two children in private school and other financial obligations that a person should even consider putting up with an abusive boss.
Insurance claim manager, male, 55

GET OUT 2

Leave. I did just that in similar circumstances. It does affect your CV – I spend more time in interviews explaining the three months I worked for a tyrant than the twenty years of employment since. However, the chap that replaced me had a nervous breakdown. That could have been me.
Finance director, male, 43

SUCK UP

Tyrants are usually suckers for some sort of exaggerated deference – find the preferred flavour, use a shovel to lay it on, ignore the remaining stress as a cost of doing business, and make good friends among the company's clients.
Lawyer, male, 56

BE A LIBRARIAN

A pedantic, condescending, political scientist? It goes with the territory. If you want a pleasant, even-tempered, monotone work environment try an accounting firm or a library.
Political consultant, male, 20s

SHARPEN YOUR ACT

Your boss may be, or seem to you, 'pedantic, condescending and patronising', but that does not make him a tyrant or a bully. The advice must be to make the most of this hard-won opportunity: learn from the criticism and prove yourself.
Director, male, 49

A JOB OFFER

Apply to Eurasia Group. We're a political risk firm and can't imagine such a disaster for a chief executive. We'd love to provide your second big job …
President, Eurasia Group

'My boss won't listen to a foreign woman like me'

ANGST ✹✹✹✷✷

DIFFICULTY ✹✹✹✹✹

> I am a foreigner who was recently relocated to work in the City of London for a leading global bank. I notice that my line manager pays no attention to my thoughts and opinions. When I share my views he looks at me as if to say: 'What rubbish are you talking?' As a result, I have stopped sharing my views with him and can feel my confidence ebbing. I am now full of self-doubt whenever I have to do something for him. What should I do?
>
> **Banker, female, 29**

THE ANSWER

I can think of four possible reasons your boss doesn't listen to you:

1. He has a general aversion to foreigners.

2. He has a general aversion to listening.

3. He doesn't rate you for some other reason.

4.   You do talk rubbish.

I'm going to skate over this last reason: if you talk rubbish you have a problem more serious than this column can address.

So that leaves the first three possibilities. As the word 'foreigner' is the only adjective you use to describe yourself, I take it that your chosen explanation is the first. Yet from the response of *FT* readers, this is controversial. Half of them disagree, thinking you a whinger and that your foreignness doesn't come into it. The other half say foreignness has everything to do with it, and many have suffered like this too.

My hunch is that the City is a rough place for a foreigner (as it can be for a woman – and you have the misfortune to be both). Yet I don't think this is the right thing to dwell on. Unless you plan to claim discrimination (which I don't recommend as it would make you bitter and a victim), I would stop trying to work out if he is anti-foreigner and instead take emergency remedial action on your tattered morale. You badly need your confidence: without it no one survives in the City.

You could resign, though I don't recommend this either as you would be leaving with tail between legs and you might not find things better elsewhere.

Remind yourself that he is just one man, and the fact that he doesn't rate you doesn't make you a useless, pathetic failure. Urgently seek out people who do listen to you, and snatch at any chance to be transferred within the bank.

Finally, comfort yourself with the second reason. Most bosses don't really listen to anyone anyway, though they go through the motions more politely than he does.

BRUTAL HONESTY

If your British manager is looking at you as if your ideas are rubbish, then rest assured he certainly thinks they are. Don't let this dissuade you from continuing to speak out. Indeed, turn it to your advantage. I have a colleague who prefaces the most outrageously brutal observations with the phrase: 'I'm sorry, I am saying what I think because I am French and I can't help it.'

Director, male, 37

ARROGANT CITY

I have a foreign name, which in Britain means I've always been seen as second class. I left the City to escape its ignorance, arrogance and mediocrity. My advice is to put all ideas in writing, find a new guardian angel at the bank, and get others to join you to abandon a dead-end manager. Mediocre managers always undermine the confidence of others.

Director, male, 57

DON'T PLAY THAT CARD

Don't play the foreigner card in London. I was a foreigner working in London for many years. People in big international companies don't care where you are from, there are millions of people in a similar boat to you – that's not why your boss is ignoring you. Find out how your boss likes people to communicate and what interests him – no point trying to engage him on a topic he does not value.

Housewife, 33

GET BUTT IN GEAR

If you conduct yourself with such a weak demeanour then no wonder you are being ignored by your manager. Get your butt in gear, have a chat with your manager and tackle the perceived issue head on. Ask yourself what have you done lately to enrich the company you work for in return for the compensation they pay you?

CEO, male, 41

ADVANCE TO GO

Play the employment game. Sue for constructive dismissal and racial discrimination. Collect £2 million. (For players outside financial-services market substitute five grand after 'collect'.)

Consultant, male, 58

LEAVE AND BE HAPPY

I am a foreigner like you; English is my third language. Your line manager does not respect you, this is not going to change – so you must leave. That's what I did and I am still a foreigner but my line manager respects me for what I do.

Manager, female, 28

❛ Should I tell my boss what I think of him? ❜

ANGST ✳✳✳✳✳
DIFFICULTY ✳✳✳✳✳

I have been asked by my boss to fill in a 360-degree appraisal form about him. He has been in the job for six months and so far has alienated most people on the team. He is an empire builder with a very high opinion of himself and he doesn't listen.

My relationship with him is superficially OK, which is why he has approached me. If I write anything near the truth on it he will work out it is me (even though the form is anonymous). If I don't, I feel I will have been a coward – and that I will have missed a rare chance to tell him what he needs to know. Any advice?

Banker, female, 34

THE ANSWER

You say this is a rare chance to tell your boss what he needs to know. It isn't. It's a (not so) rare chance to take part in one of the most unrealistic charades of corporate life. These

360-degree appraisals are hopelessly flawed, and will almost certainly have no effect on your boss's future behaviour.

The very structure of most companies makes it almost impossible to say negative things about your boss. The fact that a 'facilitator' (who will probably be no good) may stand between the two of you, massaging the feedback and making it anonymous, doesn't help much. You are right, he will probably guess who dished the dirt, and for him the discovery that you think he is an empire builder who doesn't listen will almost certainly make him think it is your behaviour that needs changing, not his.

For him to change would require that: (a) he recognises that there is a problem, which he almost certainly doesn't; (b) he wants to change it – and why should he, he has done pretty well already; and (c) that he is able to change – which is always easier said than done.

If you have a very unusual boss who really does want to know what people think of him, and who really wants to improve, then such an exercise might have some impact. But in that case, he wouldn't need a stilted, formulaic 360-degree appraisal – he'd be able to find out for himself.

I was once in a similar position with a superior, and agonised just as you are doing. I was asked to rate him on a scale of 1 to 10 on things such as vision and execution. I fudged it and wrote 5 on everything. Which I suppose was pathetic, but no more pathetic than the process itself.

That leaves you with the problem of how to deal with a less-than-ideal boss. You can't change him and you shouldn't waste time trying. Instead, you need to find a way of working with him. But if your relationship with him is superficially OK, and if he has picked you to fill out the wretched form, it sounds as though all is fine for now.

TRUTH TRANSFORMS

Ten years ago, shortly after I became chief executive, I was appraised in this way, and two of my direct reports said that I was cold and that I left my humanity at the door. I thought about it and realised it was true. I think I was trying so hard to act the part of CEO I forgot to be myself. It took a year to change my behaviour, but I think I did manage to bring more warmth to the job. You should certainly fill in the form as honestly as you can.

Retired CEO, male, 60

GO OVER HIS HEAD

You need to tell the truth, but the question is how. Find out if your colleagues feel the same way – there is strength in numbers. Then speak to your boss's boss. Tell him your concerns, give specific examples and say you want to keep it off the record. Of course, you're depending on the fact that your boss's boss isn't cast in the same mould as your boss (like tends to hire like). If this is the case, then you do have a problem!

Manager, male, 38

FIND ANOTHER JOB

Refuse to be drawn in, and respond as follows: 'Much as I think you are a splendid chap, I never comment upon my superiors as in my view it is inappropriate to do so.' Oh, and find another job, your boss sounds most unpleasant.

Senior manager, male, 60s

REVERSE KICK ASS

Your options appear to be 'reverse kick ass' or 'kiss ass'. The second might be good for you in the short term, although it may make you feel jaded at your own cowardice. Don't be afraid of the first option – if he has 'alienated most people in the team', others will probably be saying unfavourable things, too. Stand by your convictions and be honest. You may have to defend your comments, so be certain they are based on facts, not perceptions.

Accountant, female, 40s

SAVE YOUR BRAVERY

Think in pure self-interest terms, and save the 'bravery' for the football pitch or the golf course. Speaking the truth is unlikely to change him, and likely to harm you.

Banker, male, 39

UNDERLINGS

' Should I give my PA sick leave for her nip and tuck? '

ANGST ✶✶✵✵✵
DIFFICULTY ✶✶✶✶✵

> My PA recently told me that she had to go into hospital and would be off work for two weeks. I was sympathetic and told her to take as much time as she needs. I then asked delicately the reason for the treatment, to be told it was cosmetic surgery. In light of this I have said she must take the two weeks as holiday. She has responded with great hostility and is threatening to quit. I feel I am in the right, but don't want to lose her as she is efficient and pleasant and it takes time to train someone else. Help!
>
> **Manager, male, 37**

THE ANSWER

You are going to have to choose which is more important to you: having a good PA or being right. If you are even slightly sensible you'll realise that the first is more important – by a long way.

Unfortunately, you've already upset her quite badly, so you need to try to make that better. Tell her you've changed your mind and why: because you value her and don't want to lose her. Lay it on with a trowel. It is impossible to tell people too often or too enthusiastically that they are valued.

If you decide that being right is what matters to you, you are too intransigent to be a boss at all. In this case, I'm not surprised that she is threatening to resign. She probably doesn't like her job much anyway.

On the lesser question of whether in fact you are right, it is a grey area. You don't tell us what the surgery is for, which may be because you don't know. Although if that is the case, don't even dream of asking. Your questions have done enough harm as it is. If she has decided to have, say, a nose job because she feels she'd look nicer, she should surely take that as holiday. On the other hand, she could argue that her massive honker was interfering with her mental health and so the operation was as necessary as any other – although on the whole I'm with you on this.

You should also work out how you are going to behave when she gets back. A colleague recently returned from a 'holiday' with lips like a baboon. This presented a ticklish etiquette problem. I decided that the best thing was to pretend not to notice and to say nothing at all. As you know your PA is having cosmetic surgery I would ask on her return if she is fully recovered in a considerate tone of voice. Probably best not to comment on the result. And don't stare.

GOOD RIDDANCE

You've done yourself a great favour. The woman may be narrowly competent, but she isn't loyal and is deceptive, if not

outright dishonest. And rather than be chagrined by her own behaviour, she makes threats. You are lucky to be rid of her.
Consultant, female, 40s

SEND FLOWERS

Two weeks off for cosmetic surgery??!! What's she doing? A complete face-over?

You may be curious, but by asking you may already have broken the law. In most countries there are laws safeguarding privacy by which an employee taking sick leave must show proof of hospitalisation but is not required to state the reason. You have also ruined your relationship. Say sorry and send flowers to the hospital.
Risk officer, female, 36

PRETTY(ER) WOMAN 1

It is very cheeky but I think you will just have to bite the bullet and eat some humble pie. She has you over a barrel as good PAs are hard to find. Let her go and get herself nipped and tucked. Once all that swelling goes down she will look a damn sight better in the office, so it is of benefit to you too.
PA, female, 36

VANITY UNFAIR

You are quite right. If the surgery is for vanity, she must not be given time off. I assume you don't pay your employees to visit the hairdresser, gym or beauty salon – so why an operating theatre for elective cosmetic surgery?
Banker, male, 53

SHE COULD SUE

Get legal advice: you may be lining up for a lawsuit if you force her to take it as holiday because she might argue that it's necessary for her self-esteem. Depending on the advice you receive, offer her one week off as a gesture of goodwill. And remember to compliment her on her improved looks (unless it is breast enhancement, in which case better not).

Analyst, female, 30

PRETTY(ER) WOMAN 2

I had a colleague like this. She went away for a few weeks and came back after an operation where she must have lost about 10–15 kg in weight. She was a much happier and more confident person after the operation. Don't assume cosmetic surgery is only for beauty. It can also be physiological. If you get an even more efficient PA back afterwards you will be happy. Whether it should be sick leave or holiday – perhaps a 50/50 split?

Accountant, male, 40s

How do I tell my employee that he smells?

ANGST ✳✳✳✳✳

DIFFICULTY ✳✳✳✳✳

I run a small media company and have an admirable young junior member of staff who works well, is (or would be) popular and is a good team player. But he comes to work and he stinks. I don't know if it is his armpits, his clothes or his feet, but the pong is the subject of much comment in the office and is really off-putting. I think the other employees expect me to do something about it, but what? Can I get someone else to tell him or must I? And how?

Manager/director, male, 49

THE ANSWER

There is one word in your message that fills me with dread. That word isn't smell – it's small.

How small is your media company, I wonder? Is it too small to have a personnel person for you to dump the problem on? One of the beauties of personnel is they can tell malodorous workers that they must wash more carefully, and then give precise instructions and targets for how it is to be done.

Assuming that there is no such person, you have a serious problem. Such is the mad and twisted nature of managing other people that telling someone they have BO can be harder than telling them they are fired.

Partly this is because we are squeamish and were taught as children never to make personal remarks. It is also because the intimacy of what people get up to (or not) in their bathrooms is outside the remit of managers. To go crashing into this zone would be horribly embarrassing for you, and humiliating for the smeller. Worse still, after this most hideous of embarrassments, normal working relationships must be resumed. In all, it would be better for everyone if you outsource the job to someone else.

Do you have a nice deputy? Otherwise you could pick someone else in the department who can do it for you. If they handle this delicate management task, they could well deserve a promotion.

There is a slight danger that by delegating you look weak to your team. This can be avoided by explaining to the messenger that you are saving the feelings of the malodorous underling. This would be the truth – in part.

And tell the messenger that he or she must be explicit. My husband once had a problem like this and dealt with it so ineptly that he managed to offend the smeller without making him change his stinky habits.

SPELL IT OUT

It is your responsibility to tell him. Obtain some literature that explains the importance of washing your clothes and yourself every day. Sit him down and gently take him through it. Draw an analogy from smoking as smokers don't realise that they smell of smoke but everyone else does. Accentuate what a good job he does and how his problem will hold his career back if he doesn't cure it.

Finance director, male, 50s

STEALTH PONGERS

Send him an anonymous e-mail. There are many websites that can help you (some for a fee). I've done this successfully to several colleagues who have had bad breath. Doing it this way makes it less embarrassing for both of you.

Manager, female, 26

SMELL SORTED

This was how I did it. I asked the guy into my office and said that colleagues had mentioned his strong BO, and asked if he had a medical condition we should be aware of. The poor chap was very embarrassed and explained he was in a rush in the morning to get his kids ready for school and didn't have time for a shower. I suggested he use the showers in the office and also suggested deodorant. Two weeks later he popped into my office and asked if there had been more complaints and I said no, and thanked him for taking action – and that was the end of the matter.

Manager, male, 51

SMELL COVERED UP

I once had a lovely, happy woman on my team who smelled awful. I didn't say anything but got a can of air spray and freshened my office each time she left.

Executive, male, 46

DEEPER ISSUES

I know a manager who took someone aside to tell them they
smelt. It transpired that the person was sleeping rough. There
could be a very good reason for your employee's problem –
and you should get to the bottom of it now, for everyone's
good.

Manager, female, 40s

CALL THIS A PROBLEM?

This is the least problematic problem I have ever come across.
Tell him, and tell him now. I think the English suffer from this
more than other peoples – a remnant of Victorian prudishness.
How I wish all performance problems I deal with affecting
direct reports were related to easy things such as bodily
functions and not harder ones such as motivation, etc.

Trader, male, Dutch

‘ My gay PA cries at the slightest thing ’

ANGST ✱✱✱✱✱
DIFFICULTY ✱✱✱✱✱

I am a female director in a small creative agency. Over the years I've had a succession of PAs who were either thick or unreliable, but finally I have a good one. However, there is one thing wrong with him. Whenever I say anything even slightly critical he cries. Mostly he doesn't start blubbing, but his eyes fill with tears and he looks flustered.

At first I found this embarrassing but increasingly I find it enraging. He may not mean to be manipulative, but I feel manipulated – I can't raise the matter with him as I'd get the full waterworks. The situation is further complicated by the fact that he is gay. I feel that by confronting the tears I would be branded as homophobic. I think I already (unfairly) have a reputation of being a tough bitch and don't want to make it worse.

Director of creative agency, female, 52

THE ANSWER

Having a weeping PA is horrid. It is embarrassing and a bore, as it gets in the way of the work. But being a weeping PA is far worse. All dignity vanishes and the humiliation is total. Given this, your fear that he is doing it on purpose is absurd.

I've been close to tears on various occasions in the office, with eyes watery and voice wobbly. By far the kindest thing the other person can do is to pretend not to notice. This allows you to pull yourself together swiftly.

It sounds as if you are already ignoring his tears, but to no effect as his problem is chronic. To stop it you are going to have to find out why he's doing it. There are two possibilities: either something is wrong in his life outside work, making him miserable, or he is crying because you really are a tough bitch after all. Perhaps you undermine and criticise him all the time and he can't handle it.

I suggest you take him out for a drink, and ask him how he is finding things. Don't dream of mentioning the tears, but say you are worried that he isn't happy in the job. Tell him this troubles you as he is the best PA you've ever had.

Following the pep talk, experiment with being really nice. Try a moratorium on all criticism. Or if you need to criticise, do it as gently as you can.

Probably you'll find it annoying to have to tiptoe round him, but tiptoeing is surely less annoying than losing someone good and having another 'thick' PA instead.

The fact that he's gay has nothing to do with it. The fact that he's a man and you're a woman makes the tears all the more embarrassing because they are so unusual. Which makes it all the more important to find a way of stemming them.

BLUBBING ENVY

I have experienced my fair share of blubbing PAs, as well as blubbing women managers. I regard it as a strength of such women that they can express emotion in the workplace and move on. I regret that social and cultural norms have prevented me as a man doing the same. I had to make up for it outside work. I'm glad to see that one man at least does not have this inhibition.

Ex-director, male, 56

HELP FOR HIM

If he's crying it's probably because he's having a flashback to being humiliated in the past. Send him on a development course to grow into his adult identity a bit more.

PhD, female, 39

HOMOPHOBIC?

I am gay and find it absurd that you think that holding gay people accountable for their actions could be construed as homophobic. Either confront him, or don't – the fact that he is gay has nothing to do with it.

Managing director, male, 40s

HELP FOR YOU

You need a course in diplomacy to learn how to give feedback in a constructive way. It sounds like you enjoy being seen as a tough bitch. This all sounds like a self-esteem issue to me – yours. Get help!

Managing director, female, 42

YOU'RE SOFT

It's hard to believe you have a reputation of being a tough bitch when you are being so utterly soft with this character. He is shamelessly manipulating you. Keep your criticism fair, factual and free from homophobia, and make it clear you expect him to deal with it in an adult manner.

Consultant, male, 45

BE A MAN

Welcome to our world. Male managers have learnt to live with emotional female staff for centuries. Accept that you are the man in this relationship and deal with it as you would with any other over-emotional woman.

Director, male, 40

BLUB BLOG

Please don't try to sort him out. Just set up a blog and keep us informed.

Consultant, male, 50s

‘Can I fire a woman without her suing?’

ANGST ✱✱✱✱✱
DIFFICULTY ✱✱✱✱✱

I am the chairman of a small financial services company. We do not employ many women and would like to employ more. However, one of our female analysts is very weak at her job and is also unpopular with her colleagues. I would like to fire her, but am concerned that she would claim discrimination on sex grounds. Though she doesn't have a case, she is the type to push the legal point as hard as she can. I am also worried that getting rid of her might make it look as if our company is not a good place for women to work. What should I do?
Chairman, male, 58

THE ANSWER

This woman is both feeble and unpleasant. If she were just the first, then you might consider keeping her. All but the smallest companies can tolerate a dog or two. But as she is also unpopular, there is nothing for it: she must go.

However, you are right to be worried about the vindictive legal action she could take, and also right that her sex makes a big difference. If she were a man, you would simply risk being sued for unfair dismissal – and those cases do not make the headlines and the payouts they command are small.

In any event, protecting yourself against such a case is relatively easy. You can't fire anyone out of the blue for poor performance but, as long as you issue warnings and give the person a chance to get better, you can fire them after a few months when they don't.

The woman thing makes it much more risky. All she needs is to show that there might be a case for discrimination and you could find the onus of proof is on you. You would then have to show that you had not discriminated – which is almost impossible to do.

There are three things that make me fear your case is weak. You hardly employ any women, which isn't a good start. The fact that yours is a small company means you are unlikely to have sent your people on tedious, costly, diversity awareness courses, which are a legal insurance policy against this sort of thing. And if in the past you have given this woman positive appraisals then that will count against you too.

You might get away with it; you might not. If you don't and she wins her case it could not only be expensive (in the UK, at least, there is no cap on payouts in these cases), it would not look pretty to have a sex discrimination story in the pages of this newspaper.

If I were you, I would do what employers are doing quietly behind the scenes all the time. Take her to one side and offer her a lot of money, a face-saving story and a great reference, and usher her gently out of the door.

This may be costly (and distasteful in that incompetence is being rewarded) but at least you get rid of her with no ugliness and no risk.

The moral is that employers should think twice before hiring women and be sure to waste time and money on diversity courses. The whole system is less than ideal but that isn't your immediate problem.

FIRE YOUR WOMAN

We went through the same problem at a more senior level last month. I had put off the evil day, but finally booted her out and found efficiency, morale and customer complaints all improved overnight. Her female direct report came up to me and said we should have done it sooner. As for the legal niceties, we paid her off. It was the best investment we ever made – payback in less than one week.

Manager, male, 46

HIRE MORE WOMEN

Before dismissing her, I would employ at least two more women and only then start giving warnings to this female analyst.

Manager, female, 27

IGNORE GENDER

Management is no place for wimps. Get her to improve her performance or replace her. Soon. That you consider her gender speaks volumes about why your company does not employ more women. Professionals expect themselves and those around them to succeed or fail based on their accomplishments, not their gender. What you are doing now is itself sexual discrimination.

Leader, male, 50s

GIVE HER A CHANCE

Explain to her how she is underperforming (in a factual, unemotive way) and agree a plan that will bring her to the required performance standard. Document the meeting and her subsequent progress. If she persists you will have everything you need to justify letting her go. The fact that she is a woman is not relevant – or shouldn't be!

Manager, female, 40s

SECRET SEXIST

Why are you so worried about her suing over discrimination? Could it be because you know she has grounds? Why are there hardly any women in your company? In my experience the most sexist managers are the ones who claim that they champion women. I've been in the same position as this woman. I still believe I was discriminated against and wish I had taken action.

Ex-manager, female, 35

❛How do I keep my brilliant number two? ❜

ANGST ✱✱✱✲✲
DIFFICULTY ✱✲✲✲✲

I work for a big media group as head of a department that is something of a backwater. Consequently, I struggle to get my share of the organisation's talent. A year ago, I recruited a number two who is outstanding. He is full of energy and ideas, is charming to work with and seems to like his job.

Unfortunately, my boss's boss is now trying to poach him and has asked me if I think he has the maturity and people skills for a high-profile new role. I know he has both, and that he would dearly love the opportunity to prove himself. But I can't afford to lose him. Can I talk his skills down in order to keep him for a bit longer and still look him in the eye?

Manager, male, 42

THE ANSWER

I feel a little sorry for you. Not because your department is a backwater; backwaters can be perfectly nice. And not because you are losing a good number two. These things happen: bright young things never last long in backwaters.

I feel bad for you because you have made all *FT* readers instantly leap on to high horses. With one voice they disapprove of you, all bossily saying that it is your job to mentor talent (horrid phrase) and that if you even think of keeping him down you are a worm.

That's as may be. To me, the fact that you are worrying about it makes you morally superior to all the managers who routinely run down their underlings without a second thought.

Actually, your first job is not to 'mentor talent'. It is to make your department as effective as possible. Losing this guy is a blow to your department and you need to try to keep him. Not by lying, but by making a positive case to your boss's boss for why you need to keep him.

Probably he won't take any notice, because the views of those in backwaters are generally ignored. But you might win a brownie point or two.

More important, you must think about your strategy for hiring deputies in the future. Either you go for stability, which means getting someone low on gumption who is therefore happy to be in a backwater; or you go for brighter people like the guy you are losing, in the knowledge that you won't keep them long. I don't know which is better – that depends on what sort of department you run.

Either way, I urge you not to let what follows get you down.

YOU FOOL

Good grief, where to start? Is your problem really losing this guy or not being asked to move on yourself? Why are you standing at the back of the queue for talent anyway? Push up to the front or bypass the queue.

Don't restrict your employee's career or the greater good of your firm because of your Maginot Line mentality. Get a grip! Push this guy towards your boss on the explicit understanding that you will have more say in future recruitment decisions for your team. In a people business, spotting and developing good people is an important skill. Use it.

Director, female, 47

GURU VS FART

This may be a test: try to sell him down the river and the next time you look him in the eye he may be firing you – and serve you right.

I used to take pride in training people and seeing them zoom up the ladder. Praise him to the skies and you'll be seen as the greybeard guru. Blocking him will make you the sour old fart due to be put out to grass.

Ex-manager, male, 59

GLAD HEART

I do feel for you – I've faced the same issue myself. The answer is to encourage the number two to take the new post with a glad heart. It's always helpful to have friends elsewhere in the organisation, and he won't forget the one who gave him a break.

Manager, female, 45

RUTHLESS WIN

The ruthless prosper most. You have two choices: (1) Subtle: exaggerate his qualities to high heaven until your boss smells a rat or sees your chap as a threat; (2) Not so subtle: tell your boss you want something in return.

Banker, male, 56

EYE TO EYE

Wrong question. Could you still look yourself in the eye?

Director, male, 56

❝ Do I have to fire a friend? ❞

ANGST ✳✳✳✳✳
DIFFICULTY ✳

I am a director of a large company, which I joined
at a junior level ten years ago. One of my colleagues
has become a good friend – over the years we have
been on holiday together and our families know
each other. He is funny and good company, but has
grown a bit disaffected and lazy. Three years ago I
was promoted and am theoretically his boss. At first
this was fine, but now the company is downsizing
and I have to lose someone from my team – he is
by far the weakest person. I know that there are
problems in his life, and making him redundant now
would be terrible. I'm not sure I can bring myself to
do it. Equally, I can't fire someone more capable.

Manager, male, 48

THE ANSWER

Managers have to do lots of horrible things. Having to
fire people is particularly horrid, and having to fire friends

(especially ones with personal problems) is about as bad as it gets.

You have three options. You could save your friend and sack someone else – someone who works harder and better than he does. But that would be bad for them and bad for your company. And such nepotism would not endear you to anyone on your team. Alternatively, you could resign, and get out of doing anything nasty that way. But this wouldn't do either: your friend would almost certainly get fired by your successor, and you'd be in the lurch, too.

Which means – as I'm sure you know perfectly well – that you only have one course of action, and that is to do what is the right thing as a manager, and let friendship be damned.

Various readers have sent in soothing letters saying that this may be for the best in the long term. Executives who spend their lives firing people usually tell you how they were really doing the people fired a favour as they all ended up with a better job. This guff may make the executive feel better, but if you have any moral integrity, I suggest you don't offer yourself this cheap comfort. If you fire your friend you will be doing him harm. He may recover in due course or he may not.

There are two lessons to be drawn from this nasty mess, which will probably annoy you as they are easier said than done and anyway it's too late in your case. First, you should not have waited three years before talking to him about his work, as corrective action might have been possible earlier. And second, friendships in companies do not work across levels. As a manager, you can't be friends with your underlings. You have power over them and friendships founder on such uneven ground. Indeed, yours may already have done so. The 'laziness' you notice in your friend may be the side-effect of the simmering resentment that began the day you got the job.

TWIN WIN

Firing your friend may be the best thing that happened to him. I can only speak from my own experience, having been fired from my first job after graduate school. Initially I was devastated and ashamed, but it motivated me to seek out a more suitable position in which I was happier and better rewarded. See this as an opportunity for both of you.
Lawyer, female, 35

LET HIM DECIDE

Before deciding who to sack, sit down with your friend and, after discussing the situation very bluntly, lay out specific and measurable goals for him to reach over the coming months. Give him a day or two to react. If he gets in line, sack the most junior person. If he resents you, sack him. You are letting him decide his own fate.
Executive, male, 48

LET HIM HATE YOU

Been there, done that. You have to fire the person in the full knowledge that he or she will hate you and not speak to you for ten years or more. Do otherwise and the rest of the team will hate and fear you, for they will know that you are arbitrary and capricious.
Entrepreneur, male, 46

FIRE, THEN HELP

I've been in exactly the same position not once, but twice. You should fire your friend, but help him find a new job. Sell him to everyone in your network, give him a glowing reference, take time to help him think through his next steps. As to whether you are going to stay friends … all I can say is that once it worked, once it didn't.

Consultant, male, 36

PROTECT HIM

I've been in your situation and know how hard it is. If you fire your friend you do him great damage, and damage yourself too. Instead, my advice is to fire the least popular member of the group with the fewest contacts in the organisation. Before you do that, talk to your friend and explain that he has to improve since you don't know if you will be able to protect him next time.

Manager, male, 50s

WORKMATES

Should I sponsor a colleague's charity holiday?

ANGST *****
DIFFICULTY *****

A colleague has approached me to sponsor him on a charity trip in the Andes. The cause is not one I would normally support, but I am concerned that a refusal could be misconstrued as a statement either that I dislike him or that I oppose the charity, which alleviates poverty among one ethnic group. Nearly all my immediate colleagues and my superiors have agreed to sponsor the trip. However, I feel it is mostly for pleasure and that he should make his own donations.

Should I shut up and pay up, politely refuse without giving a reason, or state a reason why I am refusing – and, if so, what reason?

Stockbroker, male, 40s

THE ANSWER

This one looks hard, but is easy: you should shut up and pay up.

It isn't that your colleague deserves your support – he doesn't. He is off on a holiday, albeit one that involves a certain amount of self-flagellation. He is also being a nuisance in asking for sponsorship. It is bad enough having to sponsor the under-12s. Having to sponsor adults, especially in the office where there is the unwelcome political dimension of who gives and who doesn't, is very trying indeed.

Yet you should still pay up. Most of us don't give enough to charity, and anything that makes us give more should be tolerated. Embarrassment and guilt are powerful levers, and your colleague is pulling them to good effect.

So long as you don't actively disapprove of the charity you should grit your teeth and write the cheque, seeing it as money you otherwise would have frittered away on lattes and cab fares. The only condition is to make sure he's paying for his own trip: if he isn't, you should shame him into doing so.

If you support him, you look decent; if you don't, you look mean. The worst option is not to pay and to provide reasons. Then you look not just mean but pompous, too.

And now a personal note. Last year I went on a charity bike ride in Egypt. I couldn't bring myself to ask anyone for money, so paid half the sum myself and my employer matched the other half. Instead of feeling morally victorious I ended up feeling feeble, as many of the others on the trip had made nuisances of themselves and raised many times as much as I had.

GUILT TRIPS

These self-indulgent charity trips are the modern equivalent of a chain letter, but with an extra layer of moral 'guilt' if you fail to contribute. Be assertive, don't be blackmailed into

it. If you refuse decently you will be respected, but if you contribute you will have to answer to your own conscience.
Director, male, 50s

FACE SAVER

It's about being seen to give. While your intentions may be noble, although I suspect they are based on envy, you need to consider the longer-term consequences. Pay up with a smile, and publicly wish your colleague well. Your 'good egg' status intact, you are then free to hope he picks up a nasty tropical disease on his return home.
CFO, male, 27

TEAM SPIRIT

I work in a large company of keen, kind people, many of whom regularly undertake sponsored events that result in circulated asks for support. I put my donation down to the cost of creating a team spirit.
PR manager, female, 40s

CAN I COME, TOO?

Go with him. Really. Two weeks in the land of shamans, condors and mind-altering mushrooms – this colleague of yours is right on the money.
Banker, female, 30s

MAKE HIM PAY

A year ago I walked 400 miles from one end of Scotland to the other and raised £9,000 for multiple sclerosis. For every pound my colleagues donated, I gave the same. It sounds like your colleague can afford a similar arrangement. If you are too

embarrassed to suggest this to him, give me his e-mail address and I'll do it for you.
Investment manager, male, 50s

HE'S A PIG

Either tell him straight that you think that bloated capitalist pigs have no business tramping over the delicate ecosystem that is the high Andes or say that you donate money to charities of your own choosing and regretfully cannot support his worthy cause.
Sales director, male, 40s

BE POLITICAL

If this colleague might be important to you in the future, give some money. If you think he won't be, keep the money in your pocket and spend it in the pub. Remember, you are working, so you must never tell the truth.
Manager, male, 33

' Should I ignore my convicted former colleague? '

ANGST ✳✳✳✳✳
DIFFICULTY ✳✳✳✳✳

I used to have a business associate – a devoted family and professional man – who was convicted for acquiring child-porn pictures from the internet a year ago. He disappeared from my horizon until he contacted me a week ago by e-mail, asking me to send some material we were creating together when the catastrophe hit. My first reaction was to delete his mail at once. My second reaction was to reply and scorn him altogether. However, on third thoughts – being a female – I considered that maybe he is desperately seeking a new course in his life and contemplating his evil doings. What should I do?

Consultant, female, 40s

THE ANSWER

I have a nasty feeling that whatever you do, you will end up feeling uneasy. It seems that you used to like and respect this man – so to find that he had been downloading child porn must have been disturbing. To have him come back and ask you for a favour must be more unsettling still.

However, he is not a friend. He is not even a colleague – he is a former colleague and you have no obligations to him. One of the beauties of e-mail is that troubling messages can be easily deleted.

Still, I don't think you should do that. He has been convicted and has already been punished. There is no reason why you should punish him further. You don't need to be friendly or invite him over for supper, but you should take his professional request in the same way that you would take one from someone who had left the company under normal circumstances.

You don't say exactly what the material is that he wants. If it is something that he is entitled to, you should send it to him, possibly without any covering message. Then he will get the hint that you don't particularly want to stay in touch. If the material belongs to the company your decision is easy: do not send it.

I'm interested that you think that being a woman makes you more likely to take the soft option. I'm not sure you're right: many readers have sent in replies to your problem. Most of those were men and most of those urge you to be forgiving – or at least to hand over what he wants.

SAVE HIS LIFE

I know of a similar person who committed suicide on prosecution, leaving a devastated family. The state prosecutes criminals and persecutes paedophiles for their entire lifetimes on our behalf, so that we do not have to punish them personally. Since what he asks is not friendship and involves you in no moral conflicts, send him the material.
Ex-banker, male, 46

NOT A MONSTER?

'Child pornography' covers a broad range of crimes. A married seventeen-year-old could be breaking the law if she e-mailed a photo of herself to her husband. You should find out what actually happened before deciding what to do. You may find that the former colleague's actions, while illegal, were not those of a monster.

Consultant, male, 50s

GET TREATMENT

Paedophilia is a compulsion, not a choice to do evil. The closest you can come to your intention of assisting him is to ask outright if he is in treatment for his problem and act according to his response.

Software developer, female, 39

BANISH HIM

Your ex-colleague won't change. They don't. My advice is to reply that no further contact should be made, then block his address in your e-mail settings. All he is sorry about is being caught and having his access to children made all the more difficult.

Doctor, male, 42

HE'S NOT ALONE

Send him the material with no elaboration. He is a human being who has erred and been punished. In any large organisation there will be thieves, liars, cheats, adulterers, accountants and racists. If you were to condemn every trait you disapprove of you would be working on your own.

Manager, male, 50s

FORGIVE

Child porn has got to be among the vilest of crimes. With five children of my own, the thought turns my stomach. That said, good people make mistakes. I know it's a cliché but love the sinner and hate the sin. You may play a vital part in his recovery.

Director, male, 38

CUT HIM OFF

Delete the message. No need to get lost in the moral maze. Contact with this man will be uncomfortable, giving you unnecessary grief that, frankly, you don't need. Square things with your conscience by donating to a charity that aids the reform of paedophiles.

Journalist, female, 30s

'I fear the cleaner pinched my Nike trainers'

ANGST ✳✳✳✳✳

DIFFICULTY ✳✳✳✳✳

A week ago I spotted our office cleaner wearing an unusual pair of Nike shoes that are exactly the same as a pair I own. I had left mine in a pile under my desk but when I looked they were gone. I don't have any proof (I might have left them on the train), I don't care much about the shoes and I don't really want to get the guy in trouble. But I don't want him cleaning the office any more in case anything valuable goes missing. What should I do?

Financial PR, male, 37

THE ANSWER

You have four options, none of them terribly appealing:

1.   Confront him and ask him where he got his shoes from. I don't recommend this: even if he did help himself to your old pair, he will deny it. The conversation will be excruciating for both of you and won't get you anywhere.

2.   Report the incident to your boss (or to his), on the grounds that if you have good reason to suspect him of theft your boss should know. The trouble is that even if you are careful to say that you don't have any proof, the cleaner will almost certainly be fired without more ado. You will then have that on your conscience, which won't feel nice.

3.   You leave the cleaner alone but take better care of your things. This is superficially reasonable, though I'm still not keen. If you work in the sort of office where people leave things hanging about, that is a perk of the job. A trusting environment is a pleasant one.

4.   Do nothing at all. This is the best option, though the problem then becomes what to do with your nasty lurking suspicion. I suggest you simply squash it and let your inner liberal self (who doesn't want to get the guy into trouble) have free rein.

Comfort yourself with the thought that someone who nicks second-hand shoes and wears them under the nose of the person they took them from is not likely to be a big-time larcenist who will go for your laptop. Tell yourself that your shoes are now either in the lost property at Baker Street or on the feet of the cleaner, and that the second possibility would be better as it ensures the greatest happiness of the greatest number.

TRAINER TRASH

Didn't it dawn on you that your cleaner might have thought you were throwing the Nikes away? (The fact that you may have left them on the train shows you really don't have a clue.) Leave the poor cleaner alone – the Nikes were probably the bonus of the year for him. From the sound of things, he could

have just as easily found them in the bargain bin at the charity shop.
Travel manager, male, 38

SHOP HIM

You can't afford to have someone in the office you don't trust. As you think he stole your shoes, you have a duty to tell your boss. You never know what he could steal next. How your boss then responds is up to him. It's not your problem.
Art student, female, 20

BACK OFF

The cleaner leapt to the conclusion that you had discarded the Nikes. You've leapt to the conclusion that he stole them. Back off. Tell him that things on, around or under your desk are not cast-offs. I doubt anything else will disappear.
CEO, male, ancient

A DOGGIE TREAT?

Years ago a colleague who liked to keep chocolates on his desk decided to take action against the inevitable pilferages. He swapped them for doggie chocolate treats. It was worth it just to discover that a much-disliked manager had been scarfing the treats at night. He even pronounced them delicious. Woof! Woof!
Consultant, female, 37

LOCK UP YOUR THINGS

This one's easy. Lock up your belongings and remember that your company isn't responsible for your personal property.

Also, I'm sure your colleagues might appreciate it if you didn't keep a pile of sneakers under your desk. Eew.
Banker, male, 39

MINGING TRAINERS

Cleaners are always prime suspects for office thefts but in my long experience it's nearly all employees, with a tiny remainder down to traditional burglary. My advice is to presume the Nike-clad cleaner innocent and take personal stuff home, especially minging sportswear.
Manager, male, 45

TALK TO HIM

We dealt with a similar problem by explaining to the cleaner he was in a position of trust and it was his responsibility that none of the things in the areas he cleaned went missing. If yours has half a brain and it was him who took your trainers he will get the message, and should anything else disappear you will have just cause for dismissing him.
Freelance, male, 30s

'❝ What do I write in colleagues' leaving cards? ❞

ANGST ✳✳✳✳✳
DIFFICULTY ✳✳✳✳✳

I am getting increasingly weary about having to sign birthday and leaving cards for colleagues that seem to come round my office practically every day. Other people seem to think up funny things to say and most of the women add kisses. I can never think of anything original to say, so I usually write 'good luck' or 'happy birthday' and do not include kisses as I wouldn't kiss the person in real life. I also never know how much money to put in the envelope. For a birthday of a colleague I don't like much, I only put in a pound or two but then feel mean. Are there any rules to make this odd process easier?

Accountant, female, 31

THE ANSWER

Yes, there are rules, but you seem to know them already. It has taken me decades of pen-sucking over these wretched cards to work out that it is easy. Your colleagues may make this into a contest of lame witticisms, but you can simply opt out.

For a birthday card, here is what you say: Happy Birthday. Then you sign your name. You are right about kisses, they are not called for. These little crosses have multiplied on office cards as part of a trend to emotional incontinence. Before long 'Luv ya loadz' may be seen on office cards, so it is good to know that you and I, at least, are holding out.

Leaving cards are a bit harder, but there is a formula here, too. I have a repertoire of two comments: 'I'll miss you,' and 'good luck'. If I'm feeling extravagant, I use both. Money is hardest. However, there is no need to fret over your meanness, as it seems to be the norm. At my office the money goes into a big envelope, and so you can't usually see how much people are putting in, though if you look at the number of people who have signed the card and the amount collected it always seems low. I'm pretty sure I once saw a man slip in £5 and then remove rather more than that in change.

For birthdays I give nothing, as colleagues shouldn't expect to be showered with birthday gifts at work. With leaving collections it depends how much I like the person going. For someone I barely know and don't much like, I give a couple of quid. For someone I've worked with I give either £10 or £20, depending mainly on which notes are in my purse at the time.

The most important rule is to stop worrying. There are so many collections at work that if you fret about them all you'll never get any work done.

FRIENDLESS

People never read the comments in office cards – they just want to be reassured by the fact that all the space is full. As for the money, just think – if you were leaving, would you want a voucher worth just a measly few quid?

The bigger issue here is that you seem pretty out of touch. Try to get to know your colleagues and you'll come to see that card writing isn't quite as forensic a process as double-entry book-keeping.

PR, female, 25

TRUTH HURTS

Don't be too honest: I once had a colleague who I thought I got on with well. He wrote on my leaving card: 'I know we've not always been the best of friends but good luck anyway.' I was very upset to find out that I'd apparently been annoying him without realising it.

Anon, female

DO THE MATHS

Round your salary to the nearest 10,000, take off four zeros and that should be a reasonable contribution for a leaver with whom you worked directly. If you didn't work with the person, anything that rattles should do fine.

Anon, male

AMBIGUITY

I've used the same comment on leaving cards for more than twenty years. It's suitably ambiguous: 'Things won't be the same without you ...'

Anon, female

GIVE HALF

For birthdays, use your training, get a mortality table then write delightful messages such as '46 per cent depreciated now!'

What you write in the card doesn't matter – though make sure you enquire as to their plans and wish them well, as this will be remembered long after the (unread) card is lost. They may even offer you a job in future. Ensure no one watches you contribute your cash, then happily give half of what you consider reasonable.

Finance director, male, 50

'How do I talk to my colleague with cancer?'

ANGST ✳✳✳✳✳
DIFFICULTY ✳✳✳✳✳

Somebody who works on the same floor as me has got cancer, and I think it is bad. I don't work directly with him or even know him terribly well, but I like him and quite often share a joke with him if I meet him by the coffee machine. I know about his illness because someone else told me. I feel very awkward when I see him because I would like to say something but don't know how to bring it up. So far I have said nothing, but that feels wrong. But I can't say, 'I hope you don't die' – or can I?

Advertising executive, female, 34

THE ANSWER

A few years ago, I too had a colleague who was terminally ill with cancer. I had only ever spoken to him a couple of times, but one day I met him on the way into the office. He started asking me cheery questions about my work and I regaled him with a series of supposedly funny anecdotes.

It felt worse than uncomfortable: surreal, almost. He was dying and I didn't mention it. I never saw him again. Six weeks later he was dead.

Still, I didn't feel my stiff upper lip was wrong. By not saying anything, I was responding to what I thought was a signal from him. He had decided to work to the end and mawkish comments from near strangers were not what he was after.

The office doesn't lend itself to contemplation of death. Which is partly the beauty of it. Surely the reason that someone ill wants to go on working is to get as far away from the hospital as possible. They don't want their cancer to be the defining thing about them. This was my reasoning, and it may have been right, up to a point.

Yet now, reading the advice from cancer sufferers to your problem, I think I got it all wrong. At the very least I should have said, 'How are you?' And then he could have chosen how to reply.

The e-mails show just how differently people respond to cancer. Some want to be left alone; others don't. Some hate the silence of their embarrassed colleagues; others count on it. I won't ever know which category my poor colleague was in.

However, there is an asymmetry in the reaction which means that, when in doubt, as you are, you would do better to speak out and acknowledge that he is ill. Suppose your remark is then unwelcome, you can quickly revert to light banter with little harm done.

If, on the other hand, you say nothing to a colleague who might have been comforted by a response, the damage is greater. You look as if you either don't care or are so emotionally feeble that your embarrassment is the strongest thing about you.

A DOCTOR WRITES

I treat many cancer patients. These people do not need to be
constantly reminded that they are ill, nor do they want pity.
They live with this reality 24/7. You should continue to show
your compassion by treating him like anyone else at the office
– with a joke or interesting chit-chat. Enrich his precious time
in this way and you will not only make a difference for him,
but you will set an example for everyone else at the office.
Doctor, female, 40s

KEEP OUT OF IT

There is only one answer to your insensitive attitude:
mind your own business. I have multiple sclerosis. The few
colleagues who know are those I want to know, whom I
consider friends and whom I can trust. If your colleague has
not told you he has cancer, it is because you fall into none of
these categories.
Lobbyist, female, 30s

CALLING SPADES

I had cancer last year. I noticed that some people did not
know how to handle the issue. I was happiest with people
approaching me frankly and unpatronisingly. I did not
broadcast that I had cancer, but was willing to talk about it
openly when asked. Two in every five people in their lives will
get cancer – so you should try not to feel awkward about it.
Male, 31

PICK UP YOUR PEN

Write this man a note, and just let him know that you've
heard of his bad news. A cancer diagnosis is a heartbreak,
and it really disturbed me to know that people knew of my

cancer diagnosis through the grapevine but never picked up the phone or pen to acknowledge it. But avoid the big eyes, serious tone, 'How are you?' Everyone else does it too and it gets annoying.

Female, 40s

DYING IS LONELY

I have had cancer myself and I wanted to be able to talk about it.

Thinking about dying can be a very lonely process; it's good to have company and, as this man may not be in the office for long, it seems reasonable to acknowledge the depth of the relationship while you can.

Female, 40s

DON'T GO MAUDLIN

Ask if there is anything you can do to make his working life easier. But don't go maudlin on him.

Manager, male, 58

SEX (AND LOVE)

‘I did something silly at the office party’

ANGST ✳✳✳✳✳

DIFFICULTY ✳✳✳✳✳

I am an advertising 'suit' who has just done something unfortunate at our Christmas party. During the dinner I sat opposite the newest member of my team who is ambitious, attractive … and dangerous. She suggested the two of us went drinking afterwards, and you can imagine the rest. I am married with two young children. The next day I went into work (very hung-over!) and tried to apologise and say it was a mistake. She refused to accept that, and is clearly expecting a repeat performance. If I am any more blunt, I am worried she will seek revenge and spill the beans internally, or tell my wife. Help.

Advertising executive, male, 36

THE ANSWER

When I first read your problem I planned to be horrid in my answer. But having seen the hysterical moral indignation of some readers (see below) I now feel sorry for you.

As weak, back-sliding philanderers go, you are small beer. It doesn't sound like you've done this before and you feel guilty and realise you have a problem that you want to put right.

Unfortunately, you don't just have one problem, you have three: the wife problem, the gorgeous colleague problem and the other-people-at-work problem.

First, your wife. Don't tell her. If I were married to you (and, on balance, I'm quite glad I'm not) I'd much rather not know. The only reason for owning up would be if the 'dangerous' woman were going to tell on you. But unless she is a mad, vindictive nutter she will not do this, as it would make her look morally dodgy as well as a reject.

As for the other-people-at-work problem, it is only too probable they already know. How many of them saw the two of you staggering off drunkenly together after the party?

Yet even if they do, the damage to your prospects may be nil (hers are another thing altogether). Especially in advertising, sex with an attractive colleague is neither terribly unusual nor terribly frowned-upon.

The only really tricky thing is how you should cope with her. You are going to have to be distant and professional and stick to it. She will almost certainly respond to your new chilly style by making your life wretched. You can expect sarcastic little asides and multiple attempts to undermine you.

The best thing would be to move her to another part of the company, though this may be impossible: one false move and she could take you to the cleaners.

In all, it doesn't look pretty. And I fear the hours you spent together were not nearly good enough to justify it. Or even if they were, I am guessing that you cannot remember any but the haziest details.

COWARD AND CHEAT

It is you who is 'dangerous'. You're the one who cheated on your wife, and now you've had your way with your attractive colleague, you think it's unreasonable for her not to pretend it never happened. I suggest you tell her that you're a coward and philanderer, and that she could do a lot better. Think about telling your wife the same thing.
Journalist, female, 24

NASTY GIFT FOR WIFE

Get yourself screened for sexually transmitted infections. Having already humiliated your wife you should not make things worse by giving her an unwanted Christmas gift of an STI.
Doctor, male, 40s

ROT IN HELL

Advertising is an industry in which many senior married men think that sleeping with their young, attractive female colleagues is a fringe benefit. It is not. You deserve many sleepless nights and a stress ulcer.
Advertising executive, female, 30s

KEEP SCHTUM

(1) NEVER tell your wife. Honesty can be hurtful.
(2) NEVER have sex with anyone other than your wife again.

(3) Ignore your colleague's threats and don't be alarmed by her histrionics. Bunny-boiling is so 1980s.
Analyst, female, 45

FULL DISCLOSURE

Been there, done that, lied about it. But I don't recommend you do the same, since in your case it was a one-off, and I've found lying creates problems. You should admit all to your wife. The modern wife suspects that all her husband's office colleagues are predatory man-eaters anyway, so this will merely endorse her view. Also, own up to your boss. He/she already knows that 'Miss X' is a risk. Do it immediately and Miss X loses any 'advantage'.
Executive, male, 59

MID-LIFE CRISIS

Why did you do it? My guess is that with two young children, you feel old and responsible, and want to feel young, dangerous and desirable again. You need to deal with the underlying causes of that and get some help.
Manager, female, 34

HALF YOUR LUCK

I would love to have this problem.
Executive, male, 52

Can the sex life of one of my directors hurt my company?

ANGST ✱✱✸✸✸
DIFFICULTY ✱✱✱✱✸

I am the CEO of a large US company. I have recently received an anonymous letter containing some controversial information about one of my directors. According to the letter he has been buying sex services of an extreme and raunchy nature. The evidence includes some incriminating photographic material so I am assuming it is genuine. This director is a trusted and talented member of my team. He is well liked and well respected in the company. What he has been doing is legal and has been done in his own time without any implications for his work. I believe strongly that an individual is entitled to a private life. However, I am exceedingly concerned that if this were to get out it would impact negatively on the reputation of our company.

THE ANSWER

Yes, of course an individual is entitled to a private life. I believe that too, and so do most people – though the person who sent the pictures clearly thinks otherwise. Thanks to him your director's life isn't private any more. And unless you do something it may soon become considerably less so.

I can see that the best thing for you would be to put the beastly things into the bin and try to forget you ever saw them. Which may be quite hard next time you find yourself confronted with the man himself.

But you can't do that for two reasons. The first is that there is, as you say, some risk to the reputation of your business. It is quite sick-making that this is so, as of course his sexual proclivities should have nothing to do with the business at all. The trouble is that if the pictures are quite shocking they could well find their way into one of the more prurient newspapers on some spurious grounds or other. Although that probably wouldn't damage your company's reputation badly or for long, it would be the sort of publicity it might be nice to avoid. It depends a little what sort of business you are in – the more squeaky clean the company's image, the worse the headlines would look.

The second is the risk to the man himself, to his family life and to his reputation. I don't envy you the conversation that you are going to have with him – it's going to be horribly embarrassing for both of you. But you need to show him the letter and the pictures so that he can protect himself as best he can.

You both need to think who might have sent them. You need to think how you are going to react if they get out. You need legal advice on injunctions – not that this route did Lord Browne any good at BP.

In all I pity you. This is a wretched business, and I imagine this wasn't what you went into management for. However, if this guy is as good as you say he is, this is your chance to do him a good turn by dealing sensitively with this. You may earn his undying loyalty.

DODGY VALUES

Your director may have done nothing illegal, but he has shown a serious failure in judgement (and possibly in morality) in getting himself into this situation. You need to review if you really do need a guy like this on your executive team. In my experience of three decades of senior management, the best leaders are ones who live the company's values in their private life as well as in their working life.

Director, male, 50s

SCENARIO PLANNING

Your role as CEO means that you have a duty to protect the interests of the business and its shareholders. Consider what the impact on your company's reputation could be and how you could repair the damage. Address more than one scenario. Depending on the extent of the damage you may be better off removing your colleague from the business – any severance may be a lot cheaper for shareholders than the reputational damage. In some industries the nature of these allegations could ruin the business totally.

You should not be taking all of the burden of this upon yourself. Get some support from the chairman, other non-execs or your coach. Good luck.

Consulting actuary, male, 43

FIND THE BLACKMAILER 1

Who sent this letter and what is their motive? It could be another director or employee, in which case you could run into real problems if you are seen to have taken no decisive action. The sender clearly wants you to do something, and may take matters into their own hands if you don't.

You say you don't want to lose a talented director. Talented or not, he's clearly made one or two nasty personal enemies along the way, and you risk losing a lot more if you sit back and ignore the issue.

PR, female, 25

FIND THE BLACKMAILER 2

The real enemy here is not your director, it is the person using the director's actions to, I assume, assist them in attaining a promotion. I would keep a closer eye on his department. If you find the culprit, sack him without a second thought. He may have used this tactic elsewhere within the company. It is not the actions of your director but the saboteur releasing information about the director's activities that will damage the company's reputation.

Attorney, male

NO ONE CARES

I can't see that your company's reputation will suffer. Is BP's reputation going to be affected for Lord Browne's activities? No. If it gets out it'll be forgotten in twenty-four hours.

What would make bigger headlines would be if it is handled badly by his bosses (i.e. he is fired/disciplined in some way).

Analyst, female,30

SEX AND LIES

You seem to think that the director's buying of sex is a private matter which does not and will not affect his work. I am not persuaded of this. If this man is married/in a relationship, there is a good chance that he is lying about his use of prostitutes. Is it desirable to have a director who regularly or perhaps daily deceives someone who loves him? If he can lie systematically to one person, does that not make him more likely to lie to others?

Lawyer, male, 29

'Is my close friendship with a female colleague dangerous?'

ANGST ✱✱✱✱✱
DIFFICULTY ✱✱✱✱✱

Over the past six months I have formed a very close friendship with a female colleague. We work in the same department, share a sense of the absurd and send each other large numbers of jokey and vaguely flirtatious e-mails. Recently I've started deleting these for fear that my wife (who shares my computer at home) might see them and feel threatened and unhappy. There is nothing physical going on between us – I don't want an affair and I'm sure she doesn't either – she only got married two years ago. Yet still I am torn. I feel a bit guilty about my wife, and I think other colleagues are speculating about the nature of our relationship. On the other hand, it seems such good fun and has really rekindled my excitement for work. I don't feel like giving her up. Are there any rules to help on this sort of thing?

Manager, male, 41

THE ANSWER

I think it's perfectly possible to have a close and flirty friendship with a colleague. I've had a few of these in the last twenty years, and they have made working life a lot nicer.

There's quite a bit about your message that sounds familiar. You say that you and this woman find the same things funny – the ability to laugh at the ludicrousness of office life is the first thing I look for when choosing a new 'office spouse'. The fact that you also send each other slightly flirty e-mails also rings a bell. I've sent many of these, and highly recommend the diversion they provide.

However, there are other things in your message that don't ring a bell at all, and make me worried that you are already in far, far too deep. The very fact that you have sent me this problem is alarming. With each of my office spouses I have been able to talk to my husband about them, and it wouldn't have occurred to me to hide the e-mails. If anything I think my husband tends to feel pleased when I announce that I have a new office spouse as I come home from work slightly cheerier than I would otherwise.

But you are already chewed up with guilt. The fact that you know your wife would be jealous suggests that you know she has grounds for jealousy. Continuing in your friendship while knowing it could cause your wife pain, is proof that you are out of control in this not-so-innocent friendship. Most transparent is the way that you are grasping at straws for comfort.

The notion that she doesn't want an affair as she has only been married two years is the most pathetic excuse I've ever heard. Since when was there a time limit on affairs? I suspect that you and she are heading smartly towards an affair come what may. I suppose I should tell you not to, because it will be a disaster and will make you miserable. Worse, you may end up losing both women, living in a godforsaken flat and being denied access to your children (if you have any). Really what you should do is to retreat from her altogether, send no more e-mails and have no more cosy laughs. I daresay you could have offered yourself the same advice. But something tells me it's too late for any of that: you are already out of control. You will take no notice and do it anyway. I fear for you.

ROLL WITH IT

Flirting is what life is all about, doesn't mean you are cheating on your wife, and nor should she feel threatened.

So you've said you wouldn't ever enter anything physical with her and she feels the same, so keep rolling with it. If not, work will just get boring and your performance will suffer. In fact, your wife should be grateful that you are flirting, as it's keeping you happy in your job.

Male, 29

HAS SHE GOT A BEARD?

I think you are kidding yourself. Generally people do not flirt with each other, unless they are attracted to each other. Would you be flirting with her if she was eighteen stone and had a beard?

Based on personal experience, this can only go one way – I wish you all the best. It's going to be great fun. But for God's sake be careful with e-mails and remember to turn off your Blackberry at home.

Advertising executive, male, 44

YOUR SLIPPERY SLOPE

I've just come out of a four-year affair which started in exactly this way. I promised myself for six months that it would never progress beyond mild flirtation, but it did.

The affair was great fun, and I thought it was just an innocent bit on the side, as she was married, and so was I, and we had no intentions of leaving our partners. But eventually my wife found out, and it was very painful for everyone. I stayed with my wife, but had to deal with the fact that I was in love with my lover, and she had to deal with the fact that she was in love with me. That was probably the highest cost of the affair, and I wouldn't recommend to anyone that they pay that price.

Bottom line – ask yourself what this woman is giving you that your wife isn't, and start looking for ways to get your wife to supply that need. Or to acknowledge that your wife is actually supplying that need, but you don't give her credit for it. If you like the fantasy, then you need to ask yourself why you prefer to escape, instead of dealing with real life.
Male, anon

LOVE HER AS A FRIEND

Over the years I've had a few similar non-sexual close relationships with younger women in work. It's natural, motivating and at the time filled emotional gaps my marriage could not provide. As our lives and jobs moved on, they became good dear family friends. My advice, love your colleague for what she obviously is – a great friend.
Consultant, male, 52

DOUBLE STRIKE

First, tell your wife about her and about your fears that other people could misinterpret your relationship. That way the onus will be on her to be mature and accepting of the fact that you can have a good female friend. This will also help her put down any 'well-meaning' friends who feel it is their duty to alert her.

On the back of this, introduce your lady colleague to your wife. This is a pre-emptive strike against the little devil inside you. It should help you define your emotional boundaries and not give you the excuse that what happens at work is somehow unconnected to home life.

Manager, male, 35

DON'T, DON'T, DON'T

I've been here too – it's so exciting: the chemistry, the fun, the flirting. Result: total regret after getting totally hammered one night (easily done when you are such good 'friends'). If you've got children you really do need to get a grip and cut this affair. Don't ever tell your wife – unless you take a decision to divorce her – it'll only upset her to no purpose. But do try and rekindle the romance and excitement in your own marriage. Use your imagination and surprise her (though don't go too out of character or she'll get suspicious!).

Analyst, female, 32

ARMAGEDDON

There might be a lot of people cheering you on now, and telling you to 'just enjoy the fun'. But think about whether they're all going to be there when: (i) you have a 3 p.m. meeting with your solicitor to go through your divorce; (ii) you are selling your marital home and trying to find a scaled-down place to live; and (iii) your children (particularly if you have daughters) grow up with self-confidence issues because their dad slept with a hussy at work and destroyed their mother.

Anon

WALK AWAY NOW!

If you value your marriage and your wife at all, walk away now! I got caught up with a young woman that I supervised, rather than address the issues in my marriage. We had an emotional affair and while I never left my marriage, my wife found out and it devastated her, particularly all the lies and the fact that I thought I was in love. The affair is now over, the young woman has moved on and I did not get found out at work (I could have lost my job). However, it is not yet possible to tell whether my marriage can be saved. Was it worth it? Absolutely not! I caused my wife, whom I never stopped loving, tremendous anguish and I'm not in very good shape either. I'm angry that my wife cannot yet forgive me, and yet I'm not certain that I can forgive myself, whenever I can manage to stop justifying my actions. Indeed, I have no idea whether I can handle the difficult path of patching things up.

Senior manager, male, 49

HALF YOUR CHANCE

How lucky you are to have this 'problem' and yet so unfortunate not to enjoy it freely …

Banker, male, 34

❝ Sharing an office with my ex-lover is hell ❞

ANGST ✷✷✷✷✷
DIFFICULTY ✷✷✷✷✷

I have just finished an intense two-year affair with a colleague in the small publishing company where we both work. I ended the relationship for complicated reasons, leaving both of us feeling bitter and unhappy. It is absolute hell having to deal with him in the office every day and pretend that everything is all right. However, I don't want to leave as I have worked here for a very long time, I like the work and hours and have two kids to support. He is senior to me and could easily find another job, so I'm hoping he will leave. I know I should not have got myself into this mess. But now I don't know how to get out.
Publisher, female, 39

THE ANSWER

How do you get out of this mess? With difficulty, is the answer. First, you need to decide whether to stay or go. That depends on just how much your ex-lover wants to punish you. He is senior to you; you ended it and he feels bitter. That doesn't sound good – he could make your life so wretched that you have no choice but to go.

Assuming that he has nothing nasty planned, you should dig your heels in. Your job suits you, so you should fight to hold on to it. That means finding a better way of dealing with him in the office. You say it is awful having to pretend that everything is all right. But pretending is what you have to go on doing, and with a vengeance. You must pretend to be professional, even if you don't feel it. Get some petty pleasure by ensuring that your behaviour is always more seemly than his. If you don't have a backbone at the moment, you must develop one. Quickly.

You also need to see him as little as you can. It is a shame your company is so small or you could have moved to a different department.

Other minor changes may help. I know someone in your situation who moved her computer to remove her former lover from her line of vision, which wasn't ideal, but it was better than nothing.

Remember, though, that your colleagues have almost certainly rumbled you. Small companies are pressure cookers for gossip and they will be watching your every move.

The one thing you shouldn't do is try to make him leave. What he does is up to him. What you need to do is pretend you don't mind either way, and one day that might even be true.

THINK OF YOUR KIDS

What a stunning portrait of selfishness. The time to think of your two children was before you started an affair at your publishing office, not afterwards. Who was caring for them while you were being 'intense' with your colleague? You

wanted an affair, you had it. You wanted to end it, you did it. You don't like the guilt and tension from the 'complicated' way you went about breaking up and now you expect him to just disappear? No. For once, assume responsibility for your actions and YOU get out.
Author, male, 35

IT WAS OK FOR ME …

I had a secret affair with a colleague senior to me that lasted almost a year. When I decided to finish it we both acted maturely and carried on with our jobs as if nothing had ever happened between us. I still fancy him and when I bump into him in the lift or our eyes meet during a board meeting I still get a high, which brightens up my otherwise routine job.
Manager and single mother, 42

… AND FOR ME

There is always only one way out – through the door. So the real question is who has to go? If you are feeling guilty, you should go. If you think that you have done the right thing, let him go, or wait for a while.

Time is always the best medicine for such workplace dramas. And, surprisingly, it never takes too long to work.
Ex-boss who has been there (and did not leave), male, 52

BE A GROWN UP

You're both adults, but neither of you is mature. You need to grow up and realise you made a mistake by having an affair and the best way to correct it is to be ethical and professional at work, period.
Administrative assistant, female, 47

I MARRIED HIM

I pity your co-workers who have to work with two people who first loved and now hate each other. I know what I am talking about: I am married to a man who used to be my colleague. We both got new jobs soon after we started going out – which saved the relationship and our careers. You have to learn the hard way: love and work do not mix.

Investment banker, female, 43

TIME HEALS

Endure, it will get better.

Student, male, 33

' Why do I have to choose between love and interesting work? '

ANGST *****
DIFFICULTY **＊＊＊

Two years ago I started a new job as a management trainee at a well-known company. The job is great and I've been told that I'm in the fast track. Recently I was offered the most sought-after posting for recent trainees – a year's stint in our New York office working on a very exciting new project. This is completely my ideal job, but my difficulty is that it would mean leaving my boyfriend behind. We haven't been going out for long, and I fear our relationship won't survive a twelve-month absence. He is a junior hospital doctor who works very long hours and so won't be able to come to see me in New York at all. He says he's sure we can work something out, and says I should do it, but I'm not sure. Part of me wants to tell my boss the truth, but I fear it will make me look really drippy and as if I'm not committed. This isn't fair – I am committed to my job, but I don't see why I should be put in the position where I have to choose between love and interesting work. Surely I should be able to have both?

Management trainee, female, 24

THE ANSWER

No, you can't always have both. At least, some people manage it, but most don't. And most people – women in particular – spend their lives having to chose: job or love/ family etc.

All these decisions are wretched and there are no right answers. In your case there are so many uncertainties: is this lovely doctor going to go on being so keen when you are 3,000 miles away? Is the ideal job in New York really going to be ideal? You don't know the answers to these, and I've got even less idea.

The real question to ask yourself is: which is harder to find, a good man or a good job? Both are devilish hard, but in my experience a good man is harder. If you have a good job with a big multinational, you could switch to another big multinational and find it was much the same. With men the same does not apply: some are very much nicer than others, and a really good one is worth keeping.

Quite possibly your relationship will survive New York, though equally it might not. To say that if it doesn't, it would have failed anyway is strange reasoning to me.

Actually you aren't choosing between that. You are choosing between a good man and a slightly less fast-track job, or a fast-track job with possibly no man at all.

And if you stay, you are not giving up your job altogether, you are just giving up one opportunity now. That won't close all doors for ever.

As for what your boss will think, maybe he will think you are wimpy, and maybe your career will suffer a bit. But he is not going to fire you. You surely can try to design for yourself the sort of career that does suit you. Work hard in London and continue to please. If the relationship fails, you have missed New York this time. But I don't see why there shouldn't be more foreign postings for you later.

One proviso. All this depends on you being good at picking men. I am assuming this doctor isn't the latest in a series of giant passions that have burnt out with indecent speed? If he is, go to New York and don't look back.

ALL AT SEA

If you were a sailor, there would be no question – shipping out for a year is part of the job. With globalisation, we're all sailors to a degree. I turned down a management position abroad to be with a woman. We broke up six months later. The Russian poet Yesenin once wrote, 'From love no one demands promises'. At least your employer will provide you with a contract.

Analyst, male, 29

TAKE THE JOB

Your boyfriend will be too busy to meet anyone else, and you'll be too busy securing an exciting future for yourself to worry about what twelve months of distance might do to your relationship.

If he's a good enough man to support you pursuing your goals as he pursues his, take advantage of that because there are still a lot of men who won't go near a woman who isn't inclined to make her goals take second place to his. Live it up and take New York by storm.

Anon, female

YOU DRIP

This IS drippy. Tough choices are part of growing up.
What you're asking for is a physical impossibility, given the constraints you've presented.

You sound like someone who also thinks life owes her a right to be a full-time mother without it affecting her career, no matter how much everyone else has to bend around this. Not all constraints are due to evil bosses or discrimination. When you come up against the number of hours in the day and physical limits, you have to start making choices.

You need to work out what you want from the situation, then go after it. Telling your boss it's a really bad time for you and you want to do it next year is reasonable – as long as you make your decision, present it clearly and stop whining about life not being fair.

Banker, male, 26

WORK HARD AT LOVE

I just spent seven months away from my boyfriend with the only contact being twice weekly phone calls over the internet. Neither of us knew when we could see each other but both of us knew we wanted to be together. I'm going away again in a couple of months for another year, possibly two. This time we have the two key issues for any long-distance relationship sorted out. (1) We have a long-term plan: I move here, he moves there … (2) We have our short-term visits planned – every three months. You seem to work hard at your career, why not work hard at your relationship? After all, it's a much more important endeavour than the career, no?

Anon

CAREER SUICIDE

If you turn down NY, I can guarantee you will not be on the fast track any more, but will be included in the pool who won't be promoted beyond VP. There is no guarantee that your current BF will be your life-long partner, therefore risking your fast-track opportunity may be a very short-sighted decision. True love will survive distance and time. Unfortunately in professional life we are all replaceable and if you don't embrace the opportunities when they are presented to you, you will be left behind. There's nothing unfair about your situation, just one of the elementary tests to see if you have what it takes.
Managing director, female, 36

LIVE AND LEARN

Just recently, I accepted a similar offer for a six-month posting abroad. I had just started dating someone at that time, and I knew very well that my absence could be fatal for the relationship. And guess what? Things didn't work out. (Maybe they would have if I'd stayed at home.) Am I sorry that I took the job then? Not for a second. Even though I'm sad and bitter about the relationship ending this way, and despite the job turning out to be not quite what I expected, I don't regret making the choice I made. Even knowing then what I know now, I would still choose to go. You live, you learn.
Anon

BE HAPPY

I work in finance, and at the ripe age of twenty-three I'm already woefully tired of this corporate rhetoric that tries to convince you that a dream job can make up for a miserable personal life. My boyfriend of almost two years moved to Europe two months ago and did so only because of visa problems, but for sure we'd have worked out a compromise between his and my interests to stay in the same place if the US government didn't meddle. The advice I have to give is very simple, don't try to find all of your fulfilment in your work, you'll spend all of your time looking for it and never find it.

Finance analyst, female, 23

KICK UP YOUR HEELS

Long-distance relationships don't work. You will usually catch each other on the phone in completely different moods and times of the day, and when you're not physically with each other, it's hard to read each other's minds. You just end up wasting a lot of money on flights and phone calls and it's simply not worth it.

NYC is one of the most exciting cities in the world. I'm afraid that, if you do the long-distance thing, you won't get to enjoy the city as much – since the other will get jealous if you are having too much fun. Plus, it's a city full of attractive single people.

My advice: go to NYC and let each other free for a year. When you come back, you can see where things stand.

Consultant, male, 28

CHILL OUT, YOUNG LADY

Why on earth would you want to work in New York? It's cramped, dirty and has a very uncouth culture. Remember today's fast-track manager is tomorrow's redundancy candidate. Ignore all this career nonsense, it's usually the least able, least interesting and most insecure people who are career chasers. Say no. More opportunities will come along – in the least expected places and times. Good luck.

Anon, male

AMBITION

' I never wanted to be a lawyer, but now I'm stuck '

ANGST ✱✱✱✩✩
DIFFICULTY ✱✱✱✱✩

I did not grow up wanting to be a lawyer, I just ended up there because I had good grades and was attracted to the big salary. I left everything in my early thirties and travelled the world for two years, but then I had to come back to law-related work to pay the mortgage. Now I'm in my late thirties and desperately want to do something meaningful. But I have obligations, have acquired a lifestyle. So I lack the courage to change completely, to give up the big salary, even though I know I could be much happier living another life … but how to get there?

Lawyer, male, 30s

THE ANSWER

You say you want your work to be 'meaningful'. I cannot think of any work I would describe that way, expect possibly farming, teaching and nursing. All office work fails this test horribly.

Your predicament says more about you than about your job – I suspect you are generally fed up with life. When I get depressed journalism seems pointless; once I perk up the job starts to seem better, too.

You need to ask yourself other, more practical things about the law. Are you good at it? Do you actually hate it? If so, why? And, most importantly, what else could you do that you would like better?

This is where you come unstuck. As you do not seem to have a fantasy (mine is about teaching maths), you would do better not to change career, but change your attitude towards it instead.

If you insist on clinging to your (optimistic) view that you would be happier in another job, try this. For the next six months live like a pauper on your handsome salary. And in every minute of spare time, actively research the other things you could do. Use your legal background to work for an NGO or do legal-aid work, or retrain as a barrister. Or consider something else altogether: become an organic ostrich farmer.

If an idea takes root, use your savings and do it. If not, make the best of your present job. Stop asking yourself what it means, or whether you are happy. Find other nice things to do when you are not working and try to enjoy the money. And if you cannot enjoy it, give it to charity.

WED A LAWYER

Speaking as an ex-lawyer, my solution was to marry one of the firm's partners and rely on his humongous income.
Entrepreneur, female, 40s

BE A FROG

A first step would be to find something else to do which is not necessarily nirvana in itself but is hopefully on the right

Tube line to it. Once you're moving, you can change and importantly you should have a better idea of what not to do. Think of it as a frog crossing a pond using lily pads, rather than making it in one hop.

Broker, male, 40s

GROW UP

If you travel the world for two years in your early thirties after having worked for a few years already, you must expect to have lost the plot when you return. Interrupting your career at that age gives the worst of impressions to a future potential employer. To remedy this, you might consider spending less time whingeing and, instead, rolling up your sleeves and starting again. In other words, grow up.

Banker, male, 50s

STATE SECRET

The solution to your lifestyle problem is such that if widely known would result in the collapse of the financial services industry. It would prompt a mass exodus that would prove devastating to the UK economy. Therefore it is not in the national interest that the solution be divulged.

Stockbroker, male, 30s

JUMP

Ten years ago I quit my well-paid job and became a photographer. My friends called me crazy. But I emerged after years of commitment to my art at greater peace with myself than if I hadn't started the journey. Art is nothing without context. The context is commitment. My advice: jump. Don't worry if the bungee cord is attached or not.

Photographer, male, 60s

LAW MATTERS

Solving the problems of clients and maintaining the legal rights of people and indeed the nation is one of the most important, interesting and challenging careers in the UK. There are few jobs as interesting or 'meaningful'. You need to count your blessings and give yourself a good talking to.

Lawyer, female, 40s

HAVE KIDS

Start a family. This may give purpose and reason to paying the mortgage.

Manager, male, 50s

'Am I pursuing a half-baked dream? '

ANGST *****
DIFFICULTY *****

I am thirty-nine and have spent most of my working life in advertising, but last year I quit to pursue a long-standing dream and took a post-graduate course in journalism. I'm now working for a big media organisation as an intern (the oldest intern in the world!).

Last week I was offered a senior, well-paid job in a prestigious advertising agency doing the kind of thing I used to do (though at a higher level). The problem is that advertising is a draining and not very edifying industry to work in. Yet, if I pursue the journalism I'll continue to be a low-paid junior although I'll feel better about saying what I do for a living. I can't help thinking I'm too old and not as sprightly and energetic as I once was to make a go of it as a journalist.

I'm worried that I'm reacting to a mid-life crisis by pursuing half-baked dreams. I'm fortunate to have a partner who has a well-paid job in the City, so a low income for me isn't a disaster. I feel that following my heart will take me into journalism (and little money) while following my head will lead me into advertising. Can you help?

Trainee journalist, male, 39

THE ANSWER

I am charmed at your fanciful idea that you'll be able to hold your head up in polite company as a journalist. When I tell people I'm a journalist mostly they think that I'm scum – deeply untrustworthy and badly dressed too. When I say that actually I'm a columnist the other person feigns interest and asks that most deadly of questions: 'Where do you get your ideas from?'

You say that you are too old and not sprightly enough to make it as a journalist. I fear you may be right. I am nearly ten years older than you and am both impressed and depressed by the sheer energy and talent of journalists in their early twenties who are prepared to work long and anti-social hours on a pittance. Just looking at them makes me feel tired. It also makes me thankful not to be starting out now: the competition is worse than ever, and the number of good jobs – at least in newspapers – is in permanent decline.

You ask if you are having a mid-life crisis? Yes, I can confidently say that you are. The good news is that yours is healthy and fairly harmless. You can row back to your old industry, you've also got a wife who makes lots of money, and she is likely to remain your wife as you seem to be showing no signs of lusting after the nubile twenty-year-old journalists who will be beating you to jobs.

The only point in pursuing your dream is (to mix a metaphor) to knock the stuffing out of it. The trouble is that it may take you two or three years to realise that journalism isn't as great and glamorous as you now think. And then it may be too late: the flow of grand job offers from ad land might have dried up.

Luckily there is a compromise. Take the ad job now, and do freelance journalism on the side. If you like writing, then write about what you know about: advertising. Lots of newspapers have media sections and might be only too pleased to take a column from someone who actually knows what he is talking about.

LUCKY MAN

I would love to leave my job and do something more fulfilling, but I have a wife, two children, and a mother-in-law who depend on my income, so I have to stay in finance, even though there are many things that I would prefer to do.

You have to follow your heart – and good luck!
Banker, male, 40s

DO YOU LOVE IT?

Do you really like your job in a media organisation? It's not clear. You only mention the fact that you feel better about saying what you do for a living, which isn't the same thing. If you absolutely loved your new job in journalism, then it might be worth chucking your career in advertising.

And by the way, journalism can be draining and not very edifying, either. I know very few journalists over the age of forty-five who actually like what they do. Most leave the profession before that.
Banker turned journalist, female, 30s

HAPPY JOURNO

I faced the same crossroads many years ago and chose journalism. I took a two-thirds pay cut and it was years before

my newspaper salary caught up to where my advertising salary
had been. But I made the right decision. Life is too short
to spend your days doing something you loathe. A warning,
though: print journalism is a profession in turmoil, perhaps
even permanent decline because of competition from online
media. Make sure your partner is 100 per cent behind you, or
else be prepared to accept a major decline in your standard
of living. My first newspaper job paid so little I once ran out
of money several days before my next payday and lived on
popcorn. (And by the way, I'm over fifty and still like what I
do.)

Journalist, male, 50s

SAD JOURNO

I left a solid job with promise of long-term security to come to
London and work as a journalist. Now I'm stuck in a lousy job
as a financial journalist with lousy pay and horrible cramped
office. When I dreamt of writing about African politics and
clever columns, I never thought that the market would push
me in this direction. My advice? Go back to advertising. It's
still creative, and you can definitely write on the side. Writing
on mergers and acquisitions cannot be more exciting than
putting together an advertising campaign.

Journalist, male, 30s

BLOG OFF

Take the advertising job. Write a blog. Better still, use your
blog to write at length about the advertising industry until
such time as someone takes notice and signs you up.

You could, of course, philosophise at length about doing
the right thing, but if you can't get journalistic content out of
the characters that make up the hallowed corridors of an ad
agency, you're probably not going to make Editor anyway.

Anon, male

'Should I take a junior job or wait for something better?'

ANGST ✳✳✳✳✳
DIFFICULTY ✳✳✳✳✳

For twenty years I had a fulfilling career in the City.
Last year the bank axed the business division of
which I was chief, and I have been out of work since
then. I was initially approached by headhunters
offering relatively junior jobs, which I turned down
as I had done them ten years ago.

I now resist socialising as I just cannot bear to
hear (again) the dread question: 'How's the job
search going?' Even my wife is getting worried and
my children are fed up with having to explain at
school that Daddy is still unemployed. I should
be very employable, but the genuine senior
opportunities are few and far between. Should I go
back to work in one of the 'lesser' jobs offered to
me or hang on until the right job appears (whenever
that is)?

Resting banker, male, 44

THE ANSWER

You should take a lesser job, definitely.

First, you are driving your wife bonkers.

Second, you're driving yourself bonkers: being unemployed doesn't suit you one bit. Some people enjoy jobless periods when they've got lots of money, which I assume you have. Twenty years in the City and a redundancy cheque should mean there is no financial reason for you to work – unless you are supporting three ex-wives or have a cocaine habit, which, from the tone of your message, doesn't sound likely. Instead you seem like the sort of person (just like me) who needs a job to keep them busy and to keep the fragile ego in one piece.

Third, every week you stay at home your value to a potential employer dwindles. Employers are like children who only want the very toy that another child is playing with. If another bank isn't playing with you, why should a prospective one be interested?

Fourth, I doubt if the right job exists anyway. As you say yourself, there are precious few such openings, and even if the right one is there, it will probably go to someone younger. Life is brutal, particularly in the City.

Fifth, the lesser job may not be as bad as you think. It might be nice to work with people younger than you. You might find you are a lot better than them and will get swiftly promoted. Senior jobs are quite beastly – might it be nice not to be in charge?

Sixth, you will lose no face at parties, as most people are bored rigid with what precise position you hold at such-and-such bank. Unless, of course, you only socialise with other bankers – in which case the real problem may not be your lack of a job, but your circle of friends.

Finally, you should take the job for your children's sakes. I'm slightly surprised they are embarrassed about your unemployment, given how many fathers there are at school gates of even the poshest schools. Maybe they are picking up on your distress. Or maybe they need to change their friends, too.

JOIN THE CLUB

There must be thousands of us out there. I have been made redundant four times in my career. The reality is that you, like me, will find it almost impossible to get a job at your former level. Look around at City firms and see how many staff are over forty-five. I now do freelance journalism and am setting up my own business as no one else will employ me.
Ex-banker, male, 40s

DON'T DESPAIR

When the same thing happened to me I found it really hard to adjust. My redundancy also led to my marriage breakdown. I lost confidence in my job prospects and in myself generally. Eventually, I went to business school, got a position in finance, less well paid but still at director level. Overall I am happy and have more control over my life than I ever had before. Don't despair and don't settle for second best.
Director, female, 42

MY JOBLESS DAD

A similar incident happened to my father in 1995. He too couldn't find the right job for his level of experience, and he hasn't worked since. Hopefully you won't make the same mistake.
IT manager, male, 29

BACK TO THE BOTTOM

It's tough losing a good job, and tougher starting again. I know because I've done it. From senior investment analyst on very good pay to lowly bank clerk was no fun. But I persevered, learned my new trade and became a senior manager, with only six people between me and the chairman in a leading world bank, in a job which I greatly enjoyed.
Retired banker, male, 67

YOUR POOR WIFE

I sympathise with your wife: I've been there myself. Your family wants to see that you have a plan, that you know what you are doing. It should be something that they can present to others without shame. 'He's doing a PhD', 'He is writing a book', 'He's volunteering for a charity'. Acknowledge the fact that their patience and support may be running out and do something.
Consultant, female, 33

THOSE WHO CAN, TEACH

I became a teacher.

You'll be underpaid, overworked, taken for granted and popularly believed to be none of the above. However, the job satisfaction will make up for everything that you think you have lost.
Teacher (and ex-diplomat), male, 59

‘I'm in a rut; how do I get out?’

ANGST ✷✷✷✷✷
DIFFICULTY ✷✷✷✷✷

I am a one-time ambitious go-getter who has had the life and confidence sapped out of me by a safe, dull job in the public sector. I have also grown alarmingly complacent. Couple all of that with a wife who makes a great deal of money and I have become paralysed in my current job search. I need to jump back into the private sector and reignite my career before it is too late. How can I get my groove back on?

Former go-getter, male, 40s

THE ANSWER

You've got so many problems it is hard to know what the big one is.

You say you used to be an ambitious go-getter but have been worn down by your dull public-sector job. This doesn't sound right. Ambitious go-getters don't end up in dull jobs in the public sector, so I assume you had already stopped being an AGG before you made the job switch. In which case, why did you stop being one? Was it because you realised that going and getting wasn't all it was cracked up to be? If so, why have you changed your mind now?

Then you say you are complacent. This doesn't square with you having lost your confidence. Complacent people don't feel they have lost anything.

Finding a challenging new job is a wearisome business. It means replying to advertisements, meeting headhunters, networking, dealing with failure and so on. That's hard enough when you are feeling driven, but as you are either complacent or unconfident, it's not surprising that you've made no headway.

Now for the easy bit: your successful, high-earning wife. It's always a bad business to get too competitive with your spouse in anything other than Monopoly or tiddlywinks. If she earns a lot, you should see that as a good thing that frees you to earn less. I can think of four happy couples of my acquaintance where the woman specialises in money, the man in fulfilment. These husbands are variously a part-time architect, the editor of a loss-making magazine, a crime writer and a backbench MP. In each there is an implicit non-competition clause and a feeling that the two careers complement each other.

By contrast, I know a couple where both are bankers, only she is better at it and earns more than he does. Their relationship looks increasingly dicey every time I see them. I suggest you make your complacency a virtue. You weren't meant to be a go-getter whereas your wife probably was. If you 'get your groove back on' you'll have to work the whole time and you'll probably be doing less well than your wife.

GO GET

Why not try counting your blessings – public-service jobs have plenty. The civil servant who travels in with me on the 5.33 a.m. train does so because she's on flexitime. She collects a reliable but fairly basic salary, but knows that she will never be fired and she has a huge pension to look forward to. She gets seven weeks' holiday and her flexible working has enabled her to develop her very successful internet piracy business that she runs from home and from which she supplements her income. You say you were an ambitious go-getter, so go get.
Stockbroker, male, 49

GIVE THANKS

I was in exactly your position – my wife made more money than me for a while until my ambitions got the better of me and now I am doomed to a life of hard work. Oh, how I long for those days of reading the *FT* at work, at my leisure, and taking long lunches. Be thankful for what you have.
Executive, male, 37

GET DIVORCED

To get a new career you need a strong incentive. Get divorced or get sacked and you will discover for yourself what you have to do. At the age of fifty, with a wife and children to support, I was made redundant. After fruitless efforts to get a job (too old), I became self-employed. I was ready to do anything legal for anyone who needed help, and have now had twenty-five years of a demanding, stimulating and financially rewarding second career. The idea is not patented; have a go if you dare.
Retired engineer, male, 70s

FIND A THERAPIST

You should go into therapy. I suspect your issue might be feeling emasculated by your wife or a mid-life crisis. A more competitive job won't cure feelings of unworthiness.
Consultant, female, 48

GET MORAL

There is little that is more difficult and rewarding than making a difference in the public sector – if you are really ambitious, there's the challenge. What's more, no amount of money can reach the moral high ground.
NGO adviser, male, 31

'I have been passed over for a promotion; should I quit?'

ANGST ✳✳✳✳✳
DIFFICULTY ✳✳✳✳✳

I have just missed getting a big promotion. It was
the job of my dreams and I will probably never have
another shot at it. I could stay put and get on with
my life. I like my colleagues and enjoy my work; I am
well paid; the business is thriving; and my new boss,
who beat me to the job, treats me well. But isn't that
a bit safe? I have plenty of years' work in me. I am
still ambitious and full of enthusiasm. I know I could
do a senior job – if not here, then somewhere else.
What should I do?
Manager, male, 40

THE ANSWER

So this is your problem: you like your work; you get lots
of money for doing it; you like your colleagues; your company
is successful; your boss rates you. So far this isn't shaping up
into a terribly pressing problem. In fact, given that most jobs
are tedious, most colleagues vexing, most bosses defective,

most pay packets too thin and most companies financially precarious, you are surely in the top 0.001 per cent of the population in terms of cushy numbers.

But it's not like that, is it? You applied for the job of your dreams. You nearly got it – but then you didn't. Now you have to work under the person who did get it, and I doubt the fact that he 'treats you well' makes it much easier. You imagined yourself doing the big new job, and now you are back doing the same old one with less enthusiasm. This is the problem with internal appointments. One person wins, and those who don't are the worse for the experience: they might have been happy before they applied for the job, but in losing something gets broken that is hard to fix.

I don't think it's a matter of swallowing your pride: for ambitious people such as you, the big prize is advancement, and as you can't advance where you are, you must find somewhere else to advance instead.

People who are young(ish), ambitious and enthusiastic and who have been successful so far tend to go on to be more so. I'm confident that bigger things will fall into your lap with only a certain amount of prodding on your part. As your work is so congenial, you can wait until something really good comes along.

I wonder from the tone of your message if this is the first time in your life that you have failed to get what you wanted. If I'm right, the setback may be a good thing. To stumble is good for your management skills. It also may be good for your soul. Or something.

BUCKLE DOWN

Put your disappointment behind you and work wholeheartedly for the new boss. If they are as good as you, the combination should produce excellent results, and excellent results produce opportunities.

A team of stars does better than a one-man band.
Manager, male, 50s

GET UP AND GO

If you play it safe you'll end up regretting the missed opportunity and come to resent your boss who got the job you so badly wanted. Every move has an element of fear of the unknown, but when you've made the move you'll look back with the pleasure of having taken a risk and been rewarded. I can't understand what you're waiting for.
Venture capitalist, male, 39

FIGHT DIRTY

Think of the long game, think Gordon Brown, think Machiavellian campaign to discredit the new boss and get you the top job. You have been too nice and too safe for too long. Going somewhere else is the easy way out. Stay where you are. Dig in. Think different, get out of your comfort zone, get tough, fight dirty, play to win.
Oilman, 40s

YOUR BIG EGO

The grass is never greener on the other side. Many would kill to be in your position. If you are happy with your job despite being jumped over, the problem then is the ego. Unfortunately, that never gets satisfied, it always wants more. Move if you want new experience but not for more satisfaction. Remember, fulfilment is not always found through work. There is a bigger space outside it that you must explore.

Rejuvenated (but once battered) investment banker, male, 53

CLUELESS

For someone who thought he was ready for the senior job, your inability to know your next step shows you are clueless. If you do not know what is in store for you, I offer you sympathy.

Just wait until you are dropped two or more pay grades.

Supply-chain engineer, male, 54

‘How can I be more political and still be myself?’

ANGST ✸✸✷✷✷
DIFFICULTY ✸✸✸✸✷

I've been in the workplace for twenty years and my annual appraisals suggest that I am the kind of ambitious, hard-working, team-working individual sought by most organisations. Over the past five years, however, I have missed out on two critical promotions because, according to the feedback, I am not 'politically astute' enough.

I have never thought of myself as a political animal and am wondering how to sharpen my political antennae in a way that allows me to sit comfortably in my own skin.

Manager, male, 42

THE ANSWER

Reading your problem makes my heart sink. It sinks for you (as I fear things may be worse than you think they are) and it sinks because people talk such nonsense about office politics.

First, you. You've been passed over, twice. You asked why, and were told you aren't 'politically astute' enough. This is a pathetic reason; indeed it isn't a reason at all. It is an excuse. It sounds like you've been passed over because they simply didn't want to promote you. You are a workhorse whom they are happy to continue to employ but don't really rate, at least not in a more senior role. You might try to find out the real reason, though I doubt if you will get it, as your employers have shown that honest feedback is not something that they specialise in.

Even if they weren't fobbing you off, it's still bad news. To miss out twice makes you soiled goods. Suppose you did somehow find out what specific thing you lacked and rectified it, that wouldn't be enough to save you: your superiors would have to notice the change. In my experience it's hard changing your own behaviour, but harder still to shift people's ideas about you, especially if they're negative.

Now the muddle over office politics and whether you can become more political and still be a nice guy. Of course you can: political skills aren't bad; they are essential to getting anything done. Everything that happens in offices is political. Being good at it doesn't mean you have to become a back-stabbing snake. It means being effective: reading which way things are going, and being good at getting what you want. In some companies back stabbing is helpful, but then the fault isn't political but cultural. I expect you are good at some 'political' things or else you wouldn't have held down a job at all.

So I suggest you find a company where your abilities are appreciated. Or, if that is impossible, resign yourself to where you are and don't chase further promotions too hard.

FLATTER, FLATTER

There are three time-tested tips for rising to the top of any organisation. First, never criticise people to their face – always behind their back. Second, emulate the work habits of your superiors, firm in the conviction that even if you don't learn anything worthwhile, flattery will get you everywhere. Finally, build a reputation for seeing the cup half full even if inwardly you see it as half empty.

Writer, male, 30s

PIN THEM DOWN

To be told you're not politically astute is virtually meaningless. If you asked twenty people on the street what they meant by 'political astuteness' you would get twenty different answers. Performance appraisals are generally rubbish and based on subjective, and often secret, criteria. You need to get your appraisers to come clean about the required behaviour and not hide behind a convenient, and quite possibly dishonest, screen.

Behaviourist, male, 50s

ANIMAL FARM

You remind me of Boxer the horse in *Animal Farm*. Your good-natured hard-working attitude is being abused under the camouflage of 'teamwork'. If you are genuinely capable of delivering results you must either get what you want where you are by withdrawing your labour, or move out and move on. Finally, remember that Boxer killed himself by failing to understand the true reality of his situation.

Fund manager, male, 41

STRONG, SILENT TYPE

The first lesson is to know when to shut up. It is often the gratuitous additional comments that cause problems. Become the strong, thoughtful, silent type. If this does not allow you to sit comfortably in your skin and you have to make a comment, be more thoughtful in the way you express yourself and ask yourself if you are adding anything to the discussion.

Manager, male, 40s

BACK THE RIGHT HORSE

In most cases the 'political' solution is simple – listen to what your superiors want. Put yourself in their shoes – ask yourself what are the fundamentals behind the questions and give them the information they should have and on time. And, of course, back the right horse, be pleasant but not obsequious. It's all part of the game.

Consultant, male, 51

❛I love my work, but the money is rubbish❜

ANGST ✳✳✳✳✳
DIFFICULTY ✳✳✳✳✳

I'm in a quandary. I do interesting, rewarding work at a tiny specialised consultancy. I like the hours and the people, but the pay is measly. In London, it just doesn't go far enough. I've been told by my employer that I can rewrite my own job description to make it even better, although it wouldn't mean much more money. Instead, I could go for a bog-standard analyst position with a bank, working much longer hours but with a starting salary at least 50 per cent more than I'm getting now. So my problem boils down to this: I'm twenty-seven this year; do I take the money or the job satisfaction?
Consultant, male, 26

THE ANSWER

If I were you I'd stay put. The trouble is that I'm not you, but even taking that into account I'd urge you to stay put anyway.

There are two snags for you in analysing whether to move. You don't know how important job satisfaction is to you until you try living without it, and neither do you know how good or bad a new job might be. To move is to take a risk and, for it to be wise, the odds must be compelling.

At about your age I did the same thing in reverse. I was earning a lot of money in the City, hated the job and spent much of my time crying in the loo. I swapped this for an uncertain job on a magazine on less than half the salary. Because my starting-point was so dismal, I reasoned the new position would be better. It was: much.

If you are so poor that you can't afford to eat and pay the rent, or if the absence of skiing holidays has become unbearable, you need to move. But if you are in a greyer area, wishing you had more money but prepared to struggle on, moving looks too risky. Think how lovely your current job is. You have nice colleagues, good hours, interesting work – you can even write your own job description. At a guess, I'd put you in the top 0.1 per cent of the population in terms of job satisfaction. By contrast, I know a few happy City analysts and quite a lot of miserable ones. To run the risk of being in the latter group for only 50 per cent more money doesn't seem like a good deal at all.

Of course, the ideal position is to have money and satisfaction. You are only twenty-six; you have many years in which to achieve both. In time, can you earn more where you are? Can you supplement your income with something else? Even if you can't, you should move only when your need for more money has become intolerable. That point could come if or when you have a pram in the hall – although if you have managed to marry someone with a handsome income, that will solve all problems at one happy stroke.

DON'T SELL OUT

The moment you sell out, you will never again get the
opportunity to do unique, original work. That's the kind of
work that defines you – and your future value. Carry on rising
through your boutique consultancy for as long as you can
possibly afford. The longer you work there, the more you'll get
when you go to a big, bad bank.
Director, male, 37

GO IT ALONE

Start your own consultancy. Only a business owner can
be paid what he or she is worth. You need to look on this
opportunity as an education and do whatever it takes to get
the right business experience to position yourself as a plausible
independent consultant.
Consultant, male, 40

BUY-SIDE IS BETTER

You should be able to have both money and satisfaction. Have
a look at buy-side investment firms as well – they can offer as
much (if not more) job satisfaction and pay with better hours
than an investment bank. At your age, though, the hours
should not be a priority.
Analyst, female, 30

ANALYST'S HEAVEN

You have no idea if the well-paid job in a bank is as boring as
you imagine. Plenty of mainstream banks offer a surprisingly
stimulating work environment and the choice of jobs on offer
– once you get past the initial credibility hurdle – is much

larger than that found in a small and specialised consultancy. This could be a win–win situation for you.

Banker, male, 35

ANALYST'S HELL

I recently decided to leave a promising career in an investment bank. The salary was lavish but the working hours were inhuman, social or family life was non-existent and the level of stress was intolerable. I've given it up for a job with a measly salary but one that's interesting and personally satisfying and – guess what? – I've never been happier in my life.

Ex-banker, male, 27

A HEADHUNTER WRITES

Using maximum discretion, line up job interviews with as many of the top banks as you can. When you get a job offer, tell your employers the truth about why you would consider leaving. If they offer you enough money to stay, problem solved. If not, take the best rival offer and go.

Headhunter, male, 43

'Can I be a successful leader and still be a nice person? '

ANGST ✳✳✳✳✳
DIFFICULTY ✳✳✳✳✳

Eighteen months ago I was hired out of business school by an entrepreneurial services company to set up a new division. I recruited a team of ten, and for months we worked together around the clock to launch the business on time and within the budget. It was a great time – we were a happy and focused team.

I now find that two of the people I have recruited are not equal to the job. Both are nice guys, and well liked by the others. I'm not asking what should I do: I know I must fire them, the business can't afford to carry anyone. What worries me is more general. I am wondering whether I can go on running a lean, fast-growing business and still be a nice person. If I have to do what is right for the company, the team won't like me any more. More to the point, I'm not sure I'll like myself that much either.

My bosses say that I have everything it takes to be a great leader. Last month I was given a large

bonus and a big promotion. I want to make the
company a success, but am worried about whether
I can do this and remain the decent person I have
always tried to be.

Manager, female, 31

THE ANSWER

The answer is no. You can't be a nice person and manage
a successful business. That doesn't mean that you have to
be horrible. It means you sometimes have to be unpopular
and not mind about it. It means you must put the needs of
business ahead of the needs of individual employees – which
means you may make enemies. The simple fact of leading
means that you stand in judgement over other people and
often the judgements you will pass will be ones they won't
like.

It may have been different for you in the heady early
months, but the bigger your business gets the more distance
there will be between you and the others. So give up any idea
that they will like you: they aren't your friends and shouldn't
be. Instead, what you should aim for is their respect and
understanding that the job you are doing requires you to do
horrid things from time to time. You must concentrate on
doing the right horrid things in as humane a way as you can.
And, possibly, if you do that you'll be able to go to bed at
night thinking you aren't such a beastly person after all.

The most corrosive thing that managing people does to
the character is not that it forces you to do brutal things, it
is the stories you tell yourself to make yourself feel better.
The managers that I distrust most aren't the ones who fire all
underperformers. They are the ones who fire them but then
try to persuade themselves that they have actually done the

fired people a good turn. If instead you do horrid things but understand exactly why you are doing them you will remain an honourable person, if not exactly a 'nice' one.

THE POWER OF NICE

If you are not nice to your people you will not inspire them. If you do not inspire them you will not take them with you. Management by fear and oppression doesn't work any more.
Manager, male, 36

WHAT IS NICE?

If nice is just saying nice things and creating a clubby, non-threatening sort of atmosphere, then no.

If nice is giving people the feedback they need to improve, being honest about their challenges as individuals, then yes.
Anon, male

FIRING PEOPLE IS NICE

I've generally made more mistakes by hanging onto people for too long rather than being upfront and resolving problem situations at an early stage. Your people may actually realise that they are really struggling and waiting for an opportunity to talk with you. Dealing with this swiftly is the kind thing to do. They may be much better off in another role or with another organisation.
Manager, male, 40s

FIRING PEOPLE IS HORRID

No you cannot. The two issues (being nice and doing a good job) are mutually exclusive. To be clear, you can be decent and nice in how you go about firing them and not make it personal but you can't do an effective job if you worry about how you are going to be perceived.

I've done it twice; it's not fun and what you have to keep in mind at the end of the day is how you feel about yourself.

A few years ago after firing some members of a marketing team I ran into one of them at an industry function. The nice thing that they said to me was that I never made it personal, it was a professional decision that in time they came to understand and accept. That's about the best you can hope for.

Director, male, 48

STICKS, CARROTS AND UTOPIA

Successful leadership requires you to motivate your workers towards the team goal according to one of the following:

1.   Theory X: Stick, applicable to shirkers and rebels

2.   Theory Y: Carrot, applicable to high-flyers and enthusiasts

3.   Theory Z: Neither stick nor carrot because the workers and the team are already goal-congruent.

Z is Utopia, and normally short-lived. It's where you were in the honeymoon days of building your team.

Whichever approach you take to your underperformers, and whatever your action (keep, sack, retrain), you will have done the decent thing if you are transparent and have evidence to support your decision.

Banker, male, 34

NICE – TO WHOM?

Running a business well is being 'nice' to shareholders and to your senior managers. Being 'nice' to employees who need to be fired is being 'not nice' to your employer or shareholders

– and it means you're being 'not nice' to yourself because any poor performance on your team will hurt you.

Don't forget, in this age of activist investors, if you don't do what needs to be done, someone else will impose it on you, and you can lose your reputation and your job in the process.

One more thing: in business being nice = being doormat. Decency is a more rational, profitable and noble goal and one most people still fail to achieve.

Anon, female

CHILDREN (AND WIVES)

❝ My baby is ill and my boss couldn't care less ❞

ANGST ✽✽✽✽✽

DIFFICULTY ✽✽✽✽✽

I returned to work six months ago after having my first baby. My child has been ill and I've had trouble with nannies, so I have missed some work. Most of my colleagues have been understanding, but my boss (who is a childless woman) has been very unpleasant. She has told me I must take further time off as holiday, and that if I can't sort things out I need to consider if I am in the right job. Is this legal? Is it fair? What can I do about it? She used to be a great supporter of mine – and my skills and my desire to succeed are as strong as they were.

Banker, female, 32

THE ANSWER

There is a simple truth that doting young mothers often forget: your baby is a lovely thing in your life. She is not a lovely thing in the life of your boss or your colleagues.

You say you are the same committed employee that you always were. But actually you aren't, because that person showed up to work on a regular basis, which you no longer do.

I know that coming back to work after a baby is wretched. You are torn between work and home and are probably exhausted. Sensible employers make some allowances because otherwise they lose a lot of talented employees. But this does not mean they are responsible for or care about your child.

If I were you I would backtrack massively. Drop your aggrieved this-can't-be-legal line. Your boss should not discriminate against you because you have a baby, but it doesn't sound as if she is doing that. She is merely expecting you to do your job.

You might be able to find a lawyer who would take on your case, but morally and pragmatically you'd be better advised to reassure her that you are still committed to the job and agree to taking any further time as holiday. If you do this gracefully, she might surprise you by being nice about it.

You also need to get gold-plated childcare, which probably means throwing money at it, but one of the advantages of being a banker is that you have money to throw. Yours is a workaholic industry not ideally suited to mothers. If you look around at the ones who thrive, they have two things: a real desire to work, and either multiple nannies or a willing husband.

I bridle at the idea that your childless boss hates women with babies. Maybe she does, maybe she doesn't. Either way it isn't relevant. You say your colleagues are supportive. Are they really? If they are having to do your work, I bet they grumble about it.

DISASTER RECOVERY

Having been both the childless boss and the employee with sick young children I can sympathise with both positions. If you don't have children you can't possibly imagine the juggling act that is required.

My only advice is to seek back-ups for your back-up systems for the times when everything unravels.

PR executive, female, 30s

STICK IT OUT

I had similar problems in coming back to work and was often on the verge of quitting.

My boss was like yours, childless and jealous of me. I stuck it out and last year my boss got fired. Now I do her job.

Manager, female, 34

SPOILING IT FOR US

It is self-deluding to attribute your boss's impatience to her childlessness. Her job is to ensure that the work that pays your salary (and maternity leave) is being done – it sounds like it is not. We can all be flexible in exceptional crises but sick children and difficult nannies are hardly that in the modern workplace.

If we choose to be working mothers, we must fulfil all our responsibilities, whatever the cost. (Is your child's health not worth some holiday?) Or we must accept that something must give. Please don't spoil it for the rest of us by equating motherhood with unreliability.

Mother and managing director, 47

PLANS A TO C

I pity your colleagues: I am the worker who always has to cover for the women with children and therefore can't get my own work done. I am a loving grandmother but the bottom line is that it is hard to balance work and children. You need plan A, plan B and plan C when you are holding down a full-time job with children to make it work.

PA, female, 64

I PUT MY KIDS FIRST

I am a lawyer in solo practice and a primary caregiver to twins aged two. For me, putting work in a clear secondary role makes a lot of sense – the child will cry my name and know I will be there, at 3 a.m. or now as I type.

Lawyer, male, 56

MISSING MALE

Never mind the legality, where has your partner been through all this? Times have changed for all of us and, besides, he might have a more understanding boss.

Banker, male, 30s

How do I make my wife socialise with my colleagues?

ANGST ✳✳✳✳✳
DIFFICULTY ✳✳✳✳✳

My wife won't come to corporate events with me and I am beginning to fear this might damage my career. Recently she has turned down the opera with important clients and a buffet supper at my boss's house.

She says she has more than enough to do with her own job and our four children, and doesn't want to spend a precious evening with strangers. I understand, but my colleagues and work contacts seem to think that either my wife is unpresentable or my marriage is in trouble – neither of which is true. What should I do?

Manager, male, 39

THE ANSWER

I quite understand why your wife might not want to be dragged out to supper with your boss. What I don't understand is your fear that turning up without her could hurt your career. Possibly in the Diplomatic Service a presentable wife is still an asset. But in most other jobs a man can rise all the way to the top with no one on his arm at parties.

Next time you go on your own to a corporate do, I suggest you comfort yourself by looking at how unpresentable some of the other wives are. Indeed, the main collateral damage that a wife can inflict on her husband is not by her absence but by her presence. I know of one who gets so drunk her head goes into her plate as pudding is served. One is so bitter that any client or colleague trapped talking to her feels like they have been given a toxic injection. Others offend by being dull and vapid or indiscreet. I know one who loves to tell 'cute' stories about her husband's ways with the toothpaste tube. Corporate wives can also be a liability by flirting outrageously. And even wonderful wives can be a problem if they are so funny and so bright and engaging that the husband looks a dull thing by comparison.

If you persist in your fond idea that she should be by your side, the important thing is to get her to come willingly. If you have forced her to come when she is shattered, she may be grumpy and sarky, which won't do you any good.

The answer is a voucher system – something that I've pioneered at home. She issues you with a fixed number of vouchers – say, two or three a year. You then cash them in on the occasions that really matter to you. On voucher nights she must come along and behave graciously. On other nights you accept her absence with good grace. What you give her in exchange for the vouchers is up to both of you. Cash might be acceptable, or benefits in kind such as willing and prompt accomplishment of tedious chores.

GET A NEW WIFE

Your marriage is in trouble. You need a wife who is prepared to give up one or two of her 'precious evenings' to help her husband.

Manager, male, 66

FIND A GAY FRIEND

My wife, a chief executive, constantly moans at my reluctance to attend corporate events. She now takes along a gay friend who loves any type of diversion. Maybe you should look for a similar solution.

Manager, male, 58

TART UP THE EVENTS

If your wife finds these events boring, then other wives probably do too. So why not change the style of the events? Try theatre and music, galleries, parties in very swish places. If she still won't come, change your job. A good wife is rarer than a good job!

Wife and ex-professional, 50

LEAVE HER BE

I frequently take clients to the opera without my wife, who, like yours, works. I suggest you get the message across to your colleagues that she has her own career. Correctly put, they will envy you ... especially if they are burdened with high-maintenance, non-working wives.

If you want to show them how attractive she is, put a large framed picture of her on your desk.

Banker, male, 58

PAY HER

I once worked for a company where partners were paid a
small allowance for such events. I remember my wife writing
to my boss: 'It helps a girl to smile through the occasional long
evening and keeps her in tights.'
Director, male, 56

DO A DEAL

You clearly have a demanding job; you also seem fiercely
ambitious; and you expect your wife to look after four
children; and she works. You both expect too much. Ask your
wife to commit to one evening a month. In return, you might
spend one day a month looking after your children. If she
won't agree to that, maybe your marriage is in trouble.
Managing director, male, 52

GÖTTERDÄMMERUNG!

Easy! Invite another woman, preferably a young and attractive
one. Your wife will be at your side before you can say
'Götterdämmerung'.
Fund manager, male, 45

' Can I be a workaholic and still see my kids? '

ANGST *****
DIFFICULTY *****

I am one of three directors at a small consultancy that we started up ourselves. I work long hours and travel extensively. I love my job – it is interesting and well paid – but badly miss spending time with my two young sons. I have decided to take six weeks' non-paid leave in the summer but don't know how to convince my fellow directors that my enthusiasm and determination have not diminished. Both of them are very career-minded and are focused on becoming millionaires as soon as possible. I fear they won't be remotely sympathetic.

Consultant, male, 37

THE ANSWER

You are absolutely right – they won't be sympathetic, and I'm not sure why they should be. There's no point in trying to convince them your dedication has not changed. It has changed: you are no longer dedicated enough to work during summer as you'd rather see your children.

It sounds as if you're guilty of the worst sort of parental thinking – the sort that supposes you can both have a workaholic job and be an involved father, and that your workmates should somehow be supportive of whatever you decide to do. To you, your sons are precious. To your directors, they are a nuisance.

I suggest that you present it to them in a different, truer light. Tell them that your job still matters to you very much although there are other things that matter to you as well.

Maybe you should suggest that, when the time comes to sell the business and become millionaires, you take a slightly smaller share – pro rata with the reduced effort that you've put in.

The real test will not be how the first discussion goes but how the six weeks works in practice. I have my doubts on this. First, unless yours is a company that goes all sluggish in the summer, you will miss a lot in six weeks. Second, having a huge helping of domesticity once a year may prove indigestible for you and your sons.

If I were you, I'd try something more flexible. Say that you want to go home early one day a week. Then you can see your sons for a bit and do some more work after they have gone to bed. Your best hope for a harmonious solution is if both of the other directors swiftly have children of their own and start to feel just as torn as you do now.

JUST DO IT

Your fellow directors can think what they like. You should damn the torpedoes and take summers off if that's what will make you happiest.

Manager, male, 45

HARD FACTS

Avoid nebulous concepts like 'enthusiasm' and 'determination' and go for the tangible. You should use robust reporting of real things like revenues, profitability and client satisfaction to demonstrate that you are pulling your weight.

Consultant, male, 45

MUM'S WORD

Since you didn't mention how the mother of your little darlings feels about your well-intentioned career suicide, let me elucidate.

If you really care about your boys, continue to pursue your career, which you obviously enjoy, and leave the driving to Mum. She won't want you mussing up all her good training for six long weeks anyway.

Then, when they are seven and five respectively, take them on an extended vacation and give their mother a well-deserved break.

Mother of two, 37

SUNDAY DAD

My father had a business and he put in long hours. The time I remember most is Sundays, when he would take us out to explore river banks and museums. It's those little things that will bring you closer to your kids and that they will remember for years to come.

Counsellor, male, 50

STIR CRAZY

Having stayed at home for ten years with my young children, I can tell you your idea is terrible! After ten days I guarantee you will be pining for the office.

Mother, 40

MOVE TO SWEDEN

Most Swedish managers would be able to trump you. Six weeks' paid leave between July and August is de rigueur. I suggest you relocate your company and drag your partners with you.

UK ex-pat, male, 40s

'No one wants to hire my clever daughter'

ANGST ✳✳✳✳✳
DIFFICULTY ✳✳✳✳✳

My daughter is an Oxford graduate with a 2:1 in English. She has a business degree and is bilingual in French. She is working in marketing for a small company but is looking for something better. She has applied for twenty jobs and has had many interviews but keeps getting rejected. She has asked for feedback but has had nothing useful. An internet search engine said, 'We are not obliged to give feedback'. A PR company replied, 'We thought you were very bright but not convinced you were truly committed to a career in PR'. Is there any point in asking for reasons? And what can be done to get her a job?

Magistrate, female, 52

THE ANSWER

No, there is no point in asking for feedback. Most interviewers can't or won't explain their decisions, and why should they? They are not running a careers advice service and giving reasons simply invites future lawsuits.

In any case, your daughter has already found out what she needs to know. She didn't get the job because she failed to act as if she was gagging for a career in PR. The reason, no doubt, is that she wasn't gagging for such a career. She is a clever girl and doesn't know if she will like PR for the good reason that she hasn't tried it.

Such ambivalence may be sensible, but getting a job doesn't involve sense. It involves looking about a thousand times keener than you actually are. Before her next interview she should find out as much as she can about the job and the company. This will put her far ahead of most candidates – who can't even be bothered to check the website. She would also do well to get a trusted friend to give her a dummy interview and tell her some home truths about how she comes across. If she can do this, a brilliant future awaits. I couldn't contemplate doing such an exposing thing myself, and I'm twice her age.

Some readers have suggested that your daughter's real problem is that she has a pushy mother who writes in on her behalf. I don't think you're necessarily pushy: it's horrid to watch your child fail, and the older the child the worse, as there is little you can do. My guess is you wrote for a simpler reason: you read the *FT* and she doesn't. In which case, get her a subscription. Even if she doesn't actually read it, a folded pink paper sticking out of her bag is a nice fashion accessory.

OUBLIEZ FRANÇAIS

First, forget about the French – it has not been a serious business advantage since the nineteenth century. Second, twenty applications is nothing. What sort of hit rate do you expect? Third, the fact that you are writing on your daughter's behalf suggests that she lacks the extrovert personality required for PR.

Fund manager, male, 40s

PUSHY MOTHER

Why doesn't she want to stay in her current job? Why is she looking for something better? Could it be parental pressure?

Central banker, male, 36

OXBRIDGE ARROGANCE

As an employer, I get lots of these candidates. They are bright but give me the feeling that they'll leave when something better comes along. I never offer a job to anyone who implicitly assumes our jobs are generic enough to be done by anyone with a 2:1 from a top university.

Entrepreneur, male, 37

STOP LOOKING

I graduated from Cambridge twenty-three years ago and took much too long to realise that Oxbridge doesn't fit you for jobs in most organisations. It's not part of the programme to produce people who fit in, and we make other people nervous. Your daughter should stop applying for jobs. She should work independently as a freelancer or consultant. The working relationship is more congenial and the rewards are higher.

Consultant, male, 44

IN THE SAME BOAT

This sounds familiar. I am bilingual in Russian and English, an accountant and a graduate of Oxford's Said Business School. I have an MSc and an MBA. I have spent three years applying to every investment bank in London, Moscow and New York. Still nothing.

Clerk, female, 29

WHAT DOES SHE WANT?

Twenty jobs ... search engine ... PR company: I don't think she knows what she wants to do. In my – occasionally bitter – experience, companies can spot this a mile off. She needs some decent analysis of what she wants and a trip to the careers service. It worked wonders for me.

Oxford graduate, female, 24

A JOB OFFER

She sounds just the ticket for a role I am looking to fill in my small venture capital business. How about it?

Entrepreneur, male, 53

' I'm discriminated against at work because I'm childless '

ANGST ✳✳✳✳✳
DIFFICULTY ✳✳✳✳✳

I work in a team of five people, and mostly we get along quite well together. However, increasingly I am bothered by the fact that I am the only childless one among them. I can just about put up with being left out of the conversation – they go on and on about schools and childcare, but I am fed up with having to cover for them. I always have to work school holidays. They all take time off freely for parents' evenings. I wouldn't mind if it was occasional, but it is all the time. I have lost count of the number of extra hours I have to do to help them out of a fix with childcare or illness. This year I said I wanted to take a holiday in August and was asked if I'd mind changing it as they were tied to school holidays. I backed down, as I didn't seem to have much choice.

Recently I told our boss that I felt that as a childless person I was being discriminated against. My boss (who has children of his own)

said it was company policy to be flexible towards
working parents. He also implied that my attitude
was somehow ungenerous, and that all team
members should be supportive of each other. This
conversation has made me feel a lot worse. I am now
enraged at the unfairness of it all. Is there anything I
can do?

IT consultant, female, 37

THE ANSWER

Reading your catalogue of complaints makes me wriggle
with discomfort. I am a mother of four for whom working life
is fitted around parents' evenings, childcare crises and school
holidays. And when I do show up at work I am perfectly
capable of telling colleagues just how badly my daughter's
maths GCSE revision is going. I daresay my childless
colleagues feel much as you do.

I think you have five options – none of them entirely
satisfactory:

1. You could sue. The trouble with this is that it is expensive,
tiring, time consuming and you might not win. Also, would
you want to devote so much time to being a victim? I
wouldn't.

2. You could resign. This would be silly if you like your job.
And your problem is so widespread it might be just as bad
elsewhere.

3. You could try to think of more interesting things to talk
to your tedious colleagues about. Try starting discussions on
opera, private finance initiative, Paul McCartney/Heather
Mills etc. However, I don't like your chances: a parent dead

set on discussing schools is more tenacious than the Ancient Mariner.

4. You could get a hobby and insist on taking time to do it. Again, I can't see anyone being terribly impressed that Wednesday is your upholstery night. Children have a status in companies that upholstery and salsa dancing do not.

5. You could go on moaning. I think this is the best idea. Try to do it more constructively though. Also document all the times when you have covered for others. Gather evidence. The very best hope is that you can turn your extra work to your advantage. If you are working hardest you deserve to be paid most and promoted soonest.

6. You could stop moaning and put up with it. This is also a good idea if you have it in your power to stop being cross. Indeed, so many others are so much crosser than you are that in the end the pendulum will swing away from parents towards the childless. Alas, you may be retired by then.

BORROW SOME CHILDREN

Your best bet is to declare that, after years of waiting, you have finally received approval from the authorities to adopt. Borrow some nephews and nieces and cobble together some suitably cheesy photos for your desk. Your imaginary brood will allow you to go home early, deflect extra work, banter about Swedish nannies and permit peak-season holidays (though God only knows why you would volunteer for that).
Director, male, 32

NEXT GENERATION

Children are necessary to the preservation of the species, so reasonable discrimination in favour of children and their parents is justified. Sorry.

Doctor, male, 40s

YOU'RE THE LUCKY ONE

Rejoice that (a) someone else is rearing the workforce which will make your pension investments pay out (b) you can buy out-of-season low-cost holidays (c) you can sleep in at weekends.

Tax consultant, male, 44

YOU'RE DAMN RIGHT IT'S UNFAIR

God, I sympathise. I work double my closest colleague's billable hours only to listen to her complain that the company discriminates against mothers because it doesn't count time spent on maternity leave as active service (whereupon the company, of course, backs down). We started on the same day seven years ago, and I've been doing the job for twice as long, not even counting the countless Mondays and Fridays at home, or the extra hours I have to put in to compensate. Every time I want a day off I have to provide documentary evidence two weeks in advance that the others will be there to cover for me. Every time she wants one she tells our boss the day after she's had it (whereupon a conversation about how terrible the world is for ickle kiddies ensues).

Enough is enough. You can't keep kicking the dog.

Underpaid city worker, male, 36

SUE IF YOU CAN FACE IT

You don't have a free-standing right to claim discrimination on grounds that you are childless but, if your employer continues to overburden you to compensate for its lax management of your colleagues, you will have a claim for constructive dismissal and potentially for stress-related personal injury. Legal action is really the last resort and an expensive route for most. Instead, try and have a full and frank discussion with HR or someone more senior than your manager about your treatment and the impact it is having on you. Avoid just moaning – you are much more likely to achieve a change by talking constructively and suggesting improvements.

Employment lawyer, female (with two children), 37

FILL THE HOLE IN YOUR LIFE

You have three problems: First, office talk. Why don't you bring up topics that are of interest to you and to the others? Are you so boring? Second, covering for the others. Don't you have a private life yourself? Why don't you start learning a language, join a choir, a theatre group or a dance course? Then you could say – no, I am sorry, Wednesdays I cannot stay longer, I have an important rehearsal (or whatever). Third, holidays. Put in a holiday request early and book something. When you then have to cancel, the company should bear the costs. And most important: stop whining. Your problem is not your colleagues, it is your unfulfilled life. Giving your social life some structure might even make you find Mr Right and have some offspring of your own, not despised because you have none.

Manager and mother, 38

CHEERFUL AND CHILDLESS

If childless by choice, be happy. You are selfless and your colleagues are selfish for burdening others and overpopulating the world. If childless with regret, wait. Happiness is on the way.
Retired lawyer (childless), 55

OFFICE LIFE

❛I pressed 'send' without thinking. Help! ❜

ANGST ✳✳✳✳✳

DIFFICULTY ✳✳✳✳✳

I've done something awful! I'm the manager of a growing media company. One of our most important suppliers is extremely difficult. I thought I was forwarding a particularly tiresome e-mail that she had sent me to a colleague and headed my forwarding e-mail 'VILE BITCH' followed by a string of (actually not unreasonable) criticism. Tragically, I sent it back to her instead. What should I do? We need to continue working with her. Oh God, it's so embarrassing and difficult. I need some help.

Managing director, male, 49

THE ANSWER

Oh God, indeed. I know how embarrassing and difficult this is, as I've done it myself. I once mistakenly sent an e-mail to the then editor of the *FT* in which I cruelly and unfairly parodied a conversation we had just had, making him look weak and dithering. In the split second after I pressed 'send' I aged ten years. I propelled myself straight into his office and grovelled. In the end, I think he found my beetroot face and pathetic jabbering so dreadful he felt sorry for me.

In a way your situation is less bad as she isn't your boss (most suppliers can be replaced), though 'vile bitch' is a touch extreme and will take some apologising for.

Don't dream of doing it via e-mail; pick up the phone and ring the VB herself. Be careful how you do it, though. I detect from the tone of your message a tiny note of glee, as if you think she got what she deserved and the whole thing was hilarious in a gruesome sort of way. Squash those thoughts at once, and get grovelling. There is a (tiny) chance that she will be nice about it, and you'll realise that she isn't such a VB after all.

I should warn you against some of the advice below. Don't pretend someone else did it. That will make you look worse. Don't do as some do and send another e-mail with the subject line 'VILE BITCH recalled'. When I get these I read the original one with greater zeal.

And don't use this debacle to start a general discussion about the difficulties in your relationship. Given the hand grenade you've just thrown at it, you should apologise and then take cover and hope that things settle down.

It goes without saying that you should never do anything like this again. The golden rule is not to send any e-mail unless you would be happy to see it made public. But I sense you gaily disregard this rule daily, as indeed do I. Yours sounds like the sort of organisation where loose communication such as this is part of the culture. I bet you won't ever reform, but at least try to be more careful.

PETTY AND SEXIST

The issue here is that you felt the need to bad-mouth someone behind their back, and that you did so in grossly offensive and sexist language.

If you have a problem with a supplier or anyone else, talk to them about the impact of their actions. Don't stoop to petty personal insults. You should have moved on from that kind of behaviour in your teens.

Apologise abjectly, explain that you have suddenly seen yourself in a new light and that you now realise what an awful thing it was you did. And mean it.

Consultant, male, 56

FIND A SCAPEGOAT

You have two options – 'blame and fire' or 'cards on the table'.

Blame and fire is easy. You choose the worker you can most easily afford to lose and tell the supplier that he/she was fired for using other employees' e-mail when they were not around.

Or, face the supplier. The fact is, you need her business and she is difficult. Put your views on the table and discuss them openly.

Agency CEO, male, 46

SAVED BY SPAM FILTER

Try doing nothing – with a bit of luck your obscene remarks will have been trapped in the other organisation's spam filter and will never have reached her. Or she may have such a busy mailbox that she has deleted the barbarous e-mail deeming it to be junk.

IT consultant, female, 45

TOURETTE'S VIRUS

First, send an e-mail to everybody in your address book alerting them to the possibility that your computer has been infected with the Tourette's Virus, and it may have sent out random e-mails with offensive headers. Then go straight to the toilets and wash your mouth out with soap. Shame on you.

Director, male, 37

IF VILE BITCH READS *FT*

What you should have done was write to this column saying: 'Horrible IT glitch ... superb supplier and wonderful woman ... rude words inserted by hacker ... fear that she won't accept the truth when I explain ...', hoping desperately that your compelling excuse would make it into print.

But you didn't do that. And if Vile Bitch reads the *FT*, you've blown it.

Director, male, 50

❝ Do I dare to take a lunch break? ❞

ANGST ✸✸✺✺✺
DIFFICULTY ✸✸✺✺✺

My problem is with the lunch ethic at work. None of my colleagues ever eats a proper lunch. They sit at their desks and eat a bag of crisps, a chocolate bar from the vending machine, soda, fast food or delivery. I am sure I could get the same amount of work done if I took a thirty-minute break and ate slower. But I don't feel I can go out and take a lunch break when no one else does. I work on Wall Street – I have been in my job for under a year and am one of the most junior on my team.

Banker, female, 25

THE ANSWER

I'm a huge fan of the Diet Coke, flabby sandwich and Kit-Kat lunch consumed over the keyboard. Over the years I've found that working and eating simultaneously can be a great pleasure. I also find that if I go outside for more than ten minutes at lunchtime, coming back into the office can bring on a marked morale dip.

Still, I'm not going to try to convince you of the merits of my perfect lunch: you and I are different not just in our eating habits but in the amount of freedom we have. No one cares how or what I eat, but you don't have that good fortune – yet.

In the meantime, I suggest you cut your problem into two bite-sized pieces. One is about lunch and the other is about politics. The first is easy to solve: if the Coke and Kit-Kat pick-me-up doesn't work for you, bring in something that does. If you are worried about eating too quickly, eat more slowly. Chew each mouthful thirty-three times, as recommended by Mr Gladstone – this can be done surreptitiously while at your desk.

The more intractable side of your problem is about conformity: should you disregard the prevailing workaholic culture? The answer depends on what sort of person you are. Some people get away with breaking rules, even when they are very young. They are mostly talented and have a built-in brashness: if they want a lunch break they simply take one. A few get fired, the rest (maddeningly) rise and rise.

From the anxious tone of your message I suspect you don't belong in this group. That means you should do what the others are doing. Eat lunch at your desk, work hard and establish yourself. When you've done that you may find you are senior enough to suit yourself.

If you still insist on getting out at lunchtime I have a suggestion (though I'm not sure I'd have the stomach for it myself): bring in a sporty-looking bag, grab it at midday and say you're going to the gym.

WORK, WORK, WORK

I started my career on Wall Street and learnt very quickly that your time is not your own when you are at work. Forget about taking nice lunch breaks (at least until you become a VP and only then with clients). If you want to make it in this business, there are only three things you need to know – work, work harder and work even harder (at least until you become a managing director).

Managing director, female, 44

THIS IS A PROBLEM??

This is kids' stuff. You bring good-quality food with you and eat when you're hungry. You can NOT go out to lunch if you work on the Street, period. Get used to it or find a new career.

Director, male, 40s

BLACK RASPBERRIES

Since you are on Wall Street, head over to Whole Food in Union Square and pick up a box of California Rolls. I like the cooked shrimp and avocado, rolled in brown rice. The black raspberries were good last week, too. Then when the jerks pull out the cup cakes, you set the quick-lunch standard. In true Wall Street fashion, they will ante up to keep the game going and upscale you. Bon appétit.

Consultant, female, 40s

SUCK IT UP

Do what the rest of us do on the Street: get up around 4.30 and go to the gym to work off the junk food. You're working in an industry where at any minute of the day you could pick up the phone and write the ticket that makes your year, and for that matter, that pays you much better than almost any other job/career you could find. So, bottom line, suck it up and get back to work.

Trader, male, 48

GET A BUDDY

Recently I did an internship in Canary Wharf and formed a group of like-minded interns who nipped off at noon for a half-hour break. To get round any problems of 'skipping work', I made sure I was the first one into work every morning. Worked all right; my boss put 'hard working' in my HR remit and offered me a job.

Trainee, male, 20s

POWER LUNCH

Lunch isn't for wimps, it's for building client relationships. It is high time you built up your firm's client profile through a well-structured series of working lunches. If anybody looks askance, remind them this is a people business.

Financier, male, 46

MOVE TO FRANCE ...

... One thing the French really have right is a healthy respect for lunch.

Manager, male, 42

'They all think I'm a sexist and a racist'

ANGST ✳✳✳✳✳
DIFFICULTY ✳✳✳✳✳

I am a white, British, male MBA student at a business school in the US. Recently we had our class picture taken for the school's brochure. All the women and the ethnic minorities were arranged at the front, and when the picture was published the white males were barely visible. Soon afterwards we had a class on diversity, and I mentioned that the photograph was not representative of the school and was immediately attacked by everyone. We have been taught to think logically about business and speak our minds, but it seems on diversity this is not possible. I am a meritocrat, but now I have acquired the undeserved reputation of racist and sexist. Should I have kept quiet?

MBA student, male, 29

THE ANSWER

First, the picture. No, it is not representative, but then it is not meant to be. Your business school is doing what most organisations have been doing for years: marketing themselves as they would like to be seen, that is peopled with women and ethnic minorities, usually laughing uproariously.

I doubt if this is particularly effective in making them seem any more diverse, but I don't see it as damaging either.

Indeed, I have benefited from such a photographic bias myself, as my picture appears on the masthead of the *FT* rather more often than the faces of my white male colleagues. If I were them I'd be grinding my teeth, as I doubtless would be were I you.

But this is not about teeth grinding. It is about whether you should have spoken up about it.

Of course you should. There are difficult issues here. What is the point of diversity? How is it best achieved? Is it ever appropriate to give minorities a helping hand? How does one deal with the white male who has been passed over? And what is prejudice, and what is legitimate grievance? The ivory tower of the business schools – in which everyone is briefly more or less equal – should be the perfect place to ask these questions.

The response you got says something grim both about the US (the UK reaction might have been slightly less hysterical) and about business schools. It supports the view that they are not proper academic institutions, but places to pick up a few contacts and some dubious management claptrap on the way to furthering your job prospects. Even so, I still think you probably did right, in a pointless kind of way. You may have branded yourself as a racist and a sexist but, as your classmates are not your employers, that does not matter much.

Yet you should not attempt to repeat such honesty when you enter the job market. Business is not about freedom of speech. Open discussion of diversity is taboo, and there is no sign that it is going to stop being so any time soon.

A BIGGER OUTRAGE

Do not be disheartened. Statistically speaking, you will be paid up to one-third more money throughout your career and have a significantly better chance of becoming a chief executive than your colleagues in the front row of the photo.

If you are truly concerned about fairness in the business world, those statistics are far more deserving of your outrage.
Banker, male, 34

'TWAS ALWAYS THUS

I had a similar brush with political correctness when at Harvard Business School in 1972. (Yes, it's been going on that long!) In my case it was feminism and the circumstances were similar (all the girls were at the front).

Let it go, hone your management skills and forever remember that the 'speak your mind' philosophy is for show, not for real life.
Manager, male, 50s

THE TABLE'S TURNED

You can't play the representative card now, when your ancestors failed to honour it. Try empathy with the Africans and Asians and the female multitude that have been the subject of racism and sexism for centuries.
Ex-banker (Asian), 55

WELL DONE 1

I am an American living in Europe. I am always taken aback when I return to the US and find so many American minds closed to the basic fact that diversity covers females, African-Americans, Hispanics, oh and by the way, white males too. The picture was clearly portraying a biased representation of your class, and good for you for saying so.

Director, female, 40s

WELL DONE 2

This hokum needs to be exposed for the humbug it is. Sadly, MBA schools have earned a reputation for much bogus thought that permeates the business world and smart young people like you need to challenge the worst excesses. And you, too, are in a minority – you're a foreigner. Where are their manners?

Accountant, male, 59¾

TALL AND SHORT OF IT

I'll go out on a limb and assume that the women and minorities in your class are, overall, shorter than the white males. It's common practice to put the tall ones at the back in any photo.

White male, 34

❝How do I stop panic attacks before a speech?❞

ANGST ✳✳✳✴✴

DIFFICULTY ✳✳✳✳✴

In my job I have to give presentations regularly at conferences and to colleagues, and each time I suffer from acute anxiety beforehand. Once I am talking, I know I am a great speaker, but the 'stage fright' before these events is excruciating and debilitating, and is frequently accompanied by stomach upsets and feelings of panic. The anxiety seems to be greater if I am giving a talk to senior managers or when I am speaking to people I don't know. Is there anything you can recommend?

Manager, male, 44

THE ANSWER

Judging from the size of the mailbag, it seems that you – and I, come to that – are in very, very good company. Half the *FT*'s readership appears to be irrationally petrified about opening their mouths in front of a handful of people. Which is silly when you consider the genuinely difficult and risky things most of us do every day.

I find there is only one thing that helps, and it is the most painful thing of all – practice. The more I force myself to speak in public, the less scared I get. When I gave my first after-dinner speech I had a sleepless night beforehand, spent a long time giving the speech to my bathroom mirror and to my hapless family, then misjudged the audience and the content, and had a sleepless night afterwards cringing at how badly it had gone. Since then I have slowly got better, which has made me less frightened.

Yet you seem to be in a different position: as you are good already, practice may not be the answer.

Fear is an odd thing: to speak well in public we need just the right amount of it. Too much and we dry up, too little and we can't be bothered to do our best. Your fear is not so great that it is damaging your performance, though it may be damaging you.

Drugs are one answer. I've taken beta-blockers, which help a bit, though I don't use them much for the not very good reason that resorting to a chemical solution leaves me feeling not just frightened but feeble, too.

Alternatively you could try having a near-death experience. I nearly got knocked off my bike on the way to a speech, and found that the talk was unscary by comparison. Alas, that only worked once, and would be quite hard to replicate.

An easier tip is to ensure your presentation is not first. The one before you will almost certainly be tedious – so you will only need to be mildly droll to make the audience shake with mirth out of sheer relief.

Below are further solutions. I have left out a piece of advice offered by various readers, which is that you should imagine your audience undressed, in their underwear or on the lavatory. If I had to put myself through this ordeal every time I gave a speech I would find it not just terrifying but traumatic, too.

SPEAKER'S LITTLE HELPER

I used to suffer from stage fright – in management meetings my throat used to close up with panic. All I could do was shake my head and stay silent. My solution: diazepam. A little yellow pill taken twenty to forty minutes before performing does the trick. It's (for me) totally non-addictive. Now I can speak to audiences of up to a thousand and feel a wonderful sense of liberation at being able to do what I am good at.
Ex-academic, male, 59

TO CHURCH

To combat my nerves, I volunteered to serve as a reader at my church. The first time my knees were knocking as I was so scared. Since the text is set and quite short, I got used to it and it became banal and routine to speak to a large crowd, so now at conferences I never get nervous.
Bank president, male, 50s

AUDIENCES FORGIVE

I suffer from severe stage fright before presentations. I have analysed the root cause of it and concluded that I feared people would laugh at me, and I'd be humiliated. But in more than twenty-five years I have never seen an audience laugh at or humiliate a presenter (even those who deserved it). Audiences want you to do well. Once you understand that, the fear is overcome.
Lawyer, male, 49

FIX YOUR GLITCH

Treat it like a glitch in your personal software, and get it fixed
by a suitable professional: a psychotherapist with expertise
in cognitive behavioural therapy. This will help you unlearn
irrational mental habits and replace them with more accurate
new ones. It worked for me. A list of therapists is at www.bps.
org.uk .
Entrepreneur, male, 40

UNFAIR!

At least you're a great speaker. Think about the rest of us, the
vast crowd of mediocre or poor speakers. We know why we are
apprehensive; despite the preparation and the pre-presentation
agony all we can do is struggle through.
Manager, female, 45

‘Should I join the company cricket team?’

ANGST ✳✳✳✳
DIFFICULTY ✳✳✳✳

My boss, who is a competitive sort, and not a little frightening, has sent round an e-mail asking people if they want to represent the company in a game of cricket. He has rather darkly suggested that people should send a cricketing CV to ensure that he can pick 'a strong team'.

I love playing cricket, though am not exactly county standard. I know that were I to star in a victory it may bring me to my boss's attention – all sweaty lads together etc. – and it could help my career. At the moment I am so far beneath the radar I don't think my boss even knows who I am. But my problem is what happens if I play badly, or worse, if I run my boss out?

Should I apply, and if the worst were to happen, how should I cope with the sight of him trudging back to the pavilion, pausing only to glower back at me? I'm in a spin.

Any advice appreciated.

Journalist, male, 35

I find myself so out of sympathy with you I can hardly begin to offer advice. I hate all ball games and really can't imagine why one would want to play them at all. And even if I liked them I can't imagine ever wanting to play with colleagues. I cancelled my gym membership because I found the sight of my workmates in shorts too upsetting. Still, if I have to advise you, I'd say that you should play, on the grounds that one should do the things one enjoys. However, you should also do that typically British thing of managing expectations. Say that you would be happy to be on the team, but it's been a while, and you're not sure you can remember which end of the bat you're supposed to hold. I believe David Gower said that once, and I suspect he *did* know which end to hold. Still, if you can convince everyone you are bad and then play badly they won't be surprised. And if you play well, so much the better.

If you want to use this dreadful match as an opportunity to climb the ladder, your strategy isn't very risky. As your boss doesn't even know who you are, you aren't even on the bottom rung, so it'd be hard to fall much further.

DON'T SHINE

Your real problem is not that you may play badly – but that you play too well. Imagine him going for a third-ball duck and you hanging on to score a century. It doesn't bear thinking about, does it? You should only put your name forward if your skills are complementary to his. You don't say how old your boss is, but if he is over forty-five, I'd guess he fancies himself as a batsman, if only because his back is unlikely to be up to a sustained spell of bowling. If you are a potential wicket taker, this might work well for you. Then it doesn't really matter how well you bat, although you should probably arrange to accumulate fewer runs than your boss. But then he could post a respectable score and you could ruin it all by sending down a succession of wides. Cricket is a cruel game, as Freddie Flintoff could tell you. And whatever you decide, go easy on the post-game drinks.

PR consultant, male, 53

WHATEVER

Being afraid of your boss is equivalent to being afraid of the school bully: pointless. Your suggestion that he would be impressed if you brought yourself to his attention through a sporting achievement says more about you than it does about him. So, if you want to play cricket, put your name forward. Otherwise, don't.

CFO, female, 30s

BEER AND WICKETS

All publicity is good publicity – you should take the opportunity to become better known. The key thing to do is to relax and enjoy the day. Do not, however, turn this into a big deal – the cricket is irrelevant, sharing a beer in the pub afterwards is the most important aspect of the day – your boss will remember your name and say hello in the corridor if you score a hundred or if you drop every catch.

Anon, male

IT COULD END IN TEARS

I once worked for a company in the west of Scotland, where people were very cliquey. There were always sporting activities going on but I never seemed to hear about them. That is until my last few weeks there, when the departmental football team needed a body. As a sometime player I was keen; too keen, it turns out, because I pulled a muscle in my training and couldn't turn out after all.

Manager, male, 39

JOCK TO THE TOP

I've found that sports have invariably helped my career; in fact I'd go as far as saying that my competence at sport has by far outweighed my general incompetence in the office. You get to mix in a social setting with senior people you otherwise wouldn't get to know. The only time it worked against me was when I hit my boss's backside really hard with a squash ball (he squealed like a scalded cat) and losing to another boss, who stomped off saying, 'I thought you were supposed to be good'. Morals of those stories; try not to hit your boss with the cricket ball and don't oversell your cricketing abilities.

Marketing director, male, 44

COULD BE WORSE

Chill, man; it's only a game of cricket. You're not applying to play for the England squad. And remember, we girlies always end up being expected to make the sarnies, so there's always someone worse off than you …

Consultant, female, 39

❝ Help! Do I really have to wear chinos? ❞

ANGST **✲✲✲

DIFFICULTY *✲✲✲

A new boss has recently taken over at my office and he differs from the old one mainly in what he wears. The previous boss always wore a suit but this one is much more casual – he wears linen jackets and khaki trousers and has never been known to wear a tie. I've noticed that my team mates have stopped wearing ties too and are wearing chinos and open-necked shirts instead. I object to this as (a) they look terrible; (b) they are guilty of brown-nosing; and (c) my suits are expensive and I like wearing them. So far I am sticking to my guns, but increasingly I feel that I stick out from the others. Does this matter?

Consultant, male, 30

THE ANSWER

Yes, it does matter. Work clothes are a uniform, though different institutions have different rules. It is just like school. There are some schools where the uniform is so strict that if your tie knot is a little too loose you get a detention. There are others where it is so lax you can wear what you like. However in these 'free' schools clothes are even more important to get right than in the strict ones. To be a member of the cool set you must be in just the right sort of drainpipes, while to be in the sporty set wear shiny track bottoms and so on.

With offices it isn't much different. Your old boss wisely insisted on a strict uniform, which was easy as everyone knew what to wear and everyone could look nice so long as they bought good suits. Your new boss has swept away the old code by breaking it so blatantly himself. Yet that doesn't mean he has swept away all the rules. There are rules, only they are annoyingly harder to read.

Your colleagues have decided to take no risks in interpreting the new code and are trying to dress like him. I can quite believe they look horrible – 'business casual' is a hideous phrase for a hideous look. But I don't agree that they are exactly sucking up. They are just belonging, which is a big part of what success in offices is about.

Your boss won't look at their chinos and think: great trousers, great chap, I want to promote him! Instead, he won't think about their chinos at all, which can only be good. If, by contrast, you continue in your suits, your clothes will become an issue and you will be judged for them.

If a school were to abandon its uniform and someone went on wearing it regardless, people would think it peculiar. Equally, if you are the only one in a suit people will think you, if not exactly peculiar, then conservative, formal and a stickler. Possibly this is your image and it works. If you can make a virtue of difference, go with it. Otherwise I would go out and buy the nicest smart casual clothes you can find. Keep your suits, though. I predict that the pendulum is about to swing back. In fact your boss is a couple of seasons behind the fashion. I bet your next boss will bring back strict uniform as the first thing he does.

TAKE OFF YOUR TIE

Stick to your guns. Whilst others may choose to dress more informally in the office, it is more than acceptable to continue to wear your suit. It demonstrates professionalism and, following the move to chinos in your office, your individuality. If you feel comfortable in your expensive suits then there's no reason to change. If you feel like you need to concede some ground, go crazy and take off your tie!

Female, 20s

BRING BACK THE BOWLER

Good for you, for sticking to a suit. Nothing beats going to work in fine tailoring. It would be tragic if we all had to shop in Gap for work clothes. Work is the last place you can look genuinely 1930s stylish (without the cigarette, unfortunately) – I just hope hat wearing comes back in …

Anon, male

ANYTHING GOES

I run a project team of around twenty-five people ranging in age from early twenties to mid-sixties. My dress code is simple. If people are working in our office, they can wear whatever they like, as long as it is clean, tidy and decent (I ban micro-skirts and naked belly buttons). Some of our people always wear suits, others wear jeans and sweatshirts. I don't mind and nor does anybody else.

Consultant, male, 60

DRESS UP JOY

Well, I read this at home before I left for the office and
decided to put on my finest suit, crisp shirt and tie. I even
polished my shoes. Damn, it feels good.

Manager, male, 30s

DRESS DOWN JOY

Maybe your colleagues hate wearing suits and ties and are
not brown-nosing at all – I know I was really glad when my
company went permanently dress-down … that didn't stop
anyone dressing in a suit and tie if they wanted. Just chill out.
It strikes me that you are thinking the worst of your colleagues
(and are worried they are thinking the worst of you) – what
sort of mean-minded company do you work at? Oh yes, it is a
consultancy!

Fund manager, male

ISLEY INPUT

It's not what you look like when you're doing what you're
doing. It's what you're doing when you look like you're
DOING what you're doing. Express yourself. (I believe this is
from the Isley Brothers.)

Office manager, male

EPILOGUE

How to be a DIY agony aunt

As every agony aunt knows, solving someone else's problems is easy. Solving one's own is considerably harder.

Here is a dismal story of personal problem solving as practised by me not so long ago. My problem was all about where I sit in the office. For twenty years I had been slap in the middle of an open-plan space along with everyone else. One day an office became vacant just along the corridor. It had its own window and door (and even a tiny sliver of view) and it was mine for the asking, so long as I moved swiftly. But did I really want it? I wasn't sure.

You may be thinking that on my angst scale this hardly rates as a *. But actually as I spend at least eight hours a day at my desk, it matters to get the arrangements right. And as I was in about ten different minds about it, for me the difficulty of the problem was closer to a *****.

First, I tried thinking about it.

Would I be lonely? Would I get more work done? Or would I just play more Freecell with no one to see what I was up to? Would people be offended if I moved away? Would they think I had got above myself? Would I miss out on the gossip? Would I feel important? Would that be nice or not so nice?

I mulled these over and got nowhere. The more I thought, the more confused I became.

Next, I tried writing a list of pros and cons in two neat columns. This was fine as an exercise, but failed to lead to an answer.

I then asked a couple of people what they thought. One senior colleague with his own office said, 'Yes, of course take the office.' Another said, 'It's up to you.' This was hopeless.

The following morning I heard someone on the *Today* programme saying that the old children's game of stone–paper–scissors was being used in Asia as a way of taking business decisions. So I made a colleague play with me. If he won, I would move. If I won, I would stay put. The first time he won, but I was so furious to lose at such a stupid game I made him play again and that time I won. But he said I had cheated, so we had to play yet again. It was a diverting way of passing an afternoon, but wasn't solving the problem.

In the end I stayed put, but that was because I had dithered for so long that someone else grabbed the office instead.

Writing this book has shown me that there is a better way. I should have pretended to be my own agony aunt, and used the technique in these pages. The trick is to view your problem dispassionately and unsympathetically from lots of different angles. Think what you yourself would advise someone else in this position. Then throw in half a dozen other voices. Make them as different as you can and as rude as you like. There is no need for long answers – headlines will do. So long as they capture different practical and emotional approaches to the problem, the right solution will jump out at you. You'll recognise it when you see it.

In no time at all I wrote down the following answers:

1.   You call this a problem? You are such a snivelling little git, you obviously don't deserve your own office!

2.   You sound like a gossipy sort of person. Gossipy sorts of people are happier open plan.

3.   Office life is all about politics. You can't play politics well if you are physically cut off from people.

4.   Always take an office. A sign of status is to be grabbed. People will respect you more.

5.   Take the office and have the best of all worlds. Quiet when you want it. And then, if you want to chat, you can go outside and do so.

6.   If you are perfectly happy where you are, stay put. And stop moaning.

Reading these through I find that, hey presto, my problem is solved. The first headline briefly moved me to action. I thought: sod you – I'll take the office, out of sheer defiance. But that feeling went as soon as I read view 6: If you are happy(ish) then change isn't worth it. This sounds right to me. It is exactly the advice I would have given myself.

It's a shame that I invented this DIY agony aunt tool too late for that occasion, though I am definitely going to use it in the future. I recommend that you do too: I'm sure you will find, just as I did, that writing down a handful of extreme, rude and conflicting views will jog your mind towards the right solution. But if it doesn't I have another idea, which I like even better. Send the problem to me: Problems@ft.com.